D0566800

ESSENTIAL
BLACK
WISDOM

ESSENTIAL
BLACK
WISDOM

Quotes of Inspiration
and Strength

EDITED BY
CAROL KELLY-GANGI

FALL RIVER PRESS

New York

Special thanks to Chris Barsanti for all of his guidance,
support, and expertise on the Essential Wisdom series.

FALL RIVER PRESS

New York

An Imprint of Sterling Publishing Co., Inc.
1166 Avenue of the Americas
New York, NY 10036

FALL RIVER PRESS and the distinctive Fall River Press logo
are registered trademarks of Barnes & Noble Booksellers, Inc.

Compilation © 2018 Sterling Publishing Co., Inc.

All rights reserved. No part of this publication may be reproduced, stored in a retrieval
system, or transmitted in any form or by any means (including electronic, mechanical,
photocopying, recording, or otherwise) without prior written permission from the publisher.

ISBN 978-1-4351-6852-7

Distributed in Canada by Sterling Publishing Co., Inc.
c/o Canadian Manda Group, 664 Annette Street
Toronto, Ontario M6S 2C8, Canada
Distributed in the United Kingdom by GMC Distribution Services
Castle Place, 166 High Street, Lewes, East Sussex BN7 1XU, England
Distributed in Australia by NewSouth Books
University of New South Wales, Sydney, NSW 2052, Australia

For information about custom editions, special sales, and premium and corporate purchases,
please contact Sterling Special Sales at 800-805-5489 or specialsales@sterlingpublishing.com.

Manufactured in Canada

2 4 6 8 10 9 7 5 3

sterlingpublishing.com

Cover design by Scott Russo

CONTENTS

❋   ❋   ❋   ❋   ❋

INTRODUCTION

✻   ✻   ✻   ✻   ✻

The rich tradition of oral and written wisdom from persons of African descent dates back thousands of years. In *Essential Black Wisdom* we have carefully curated hundreds of powerful quotations from an extraordinary array of men and women. There are voices from antiquity up through the present day that speak to the hopes, dreams, joys, struggles, and steadfast endurance of this great people. The contributors come from all walks of life and include writers, activists, and artists; poets, politicians, and historians; leaders, statesmen, and scientists; actors, athletes, and musicians; and many others whose words have left a lasting impact on their world and on history. Who are these great leaders? Within these pages you will find presidents and prime ministers; saints and scientists; politicians and philosophers; judges and generals; activists and athletes; investors and inventors; professors and poets; and statesmen and scholars. It is hoped that the words of these extraordinary men and women will cut across the boundaries of time and place to form an open discourse on leadership.

Of the many universal themes that emerge, there is the struggle for freedom, equality, and justice; the quest for knowledge; the fierce love of family; the need for love and kindness; and overcoming the obstacle of racism in all of its ugly guises. In other respects, the quotations are as singular as the speakers themselves. In the excerpts that follow, Frederick Douglass rails against the horrors of slavery; Desmond Tutu urges humankind to stand for justice; and Marian Wright Edelman speaks passionately about education. Muhammad Ali, Whoopi Goldberg, Kamala Harris, Toni Morrison, and Barack Obama reflect on the American Dream, while

Chinua Achebe, Lani Guinier, Nelson Mandela, and Thurgood Marshall extol the virtues of democracy. Other selections reveal a more personal side of the contributors. Maya Angelou, Martin Luther King Jr., and Harriet Tubman speak reverently about the sustaining power of faith. Hank Aaron, Marian Anderson, Shirley Chisholm, Zora Neale Hurston, Spike Lee, Jordan Peele, Cornel West, and Malcolm X share powerful insights on race and racism. Elsewhere, Ray Charles, Kevin Durant, Trevor Noah, Wilma Rudolph, and Oprah Winfrey recall with wonder the sacrifices of their mothers and grandmothers; while Malcolm Gladwell, Condoleezza Rice, and Paul Robeson lovingly remember their fathers. In other chapters, the contributors exchange their views on the legacy of slavery, the meaning of suffering, the balm of friendship, the path to success, and the need for tireless activism.

Weaving a rich tapestry of voices, *Essential Black Wisdom* invites all readers to experience the powerful words, hopeful spirit, and enduring legacy of black people through the ages.

—CAROL KELLY-GANGI
2018

KNOWLEDGE, EDUCATION, AND INNOVATION

What we have got to know, so far as possible, are the things that actually happened in the world. Then with that much clear and open to every reader, the philosopher and prophet has a chance to interpret these facts.

—W. E. B. Du Bois

Man only truly lives by knowing; otherwise he simply performs, copying the daily habits of others, but conceiving nothing of his creative possibilities as a man, and accepting someone else's superiority and his own misery.

—Alice Walker

I'm hungry for knowledge. The whole thing is to learn every day, to get brighter and brighter. That's what this world is about. You look at someone like Gandhi, and he glowed. Martin Luther King glowed. Muhammad Ali glows. I think that's from being bright all the time and trying to be brighter.

—Jay-Z

I wanted to know the name of every stone and flower and insect and bird and beast. I wanted to know where it got its color, where it got its life—but there was no one to tell me.

—George Washington Carver

I have always worshipped at the shrine of knowledge knowing that regardless of how much I study, read, travel, expose myself to enriching experiences, I still remain an intellectual pauper.

—Adam Clayton Powell Jr.

Books were my pass to personal freedom. I learned to read at age three, and soon discovered there was a whole world to conquer that went beyond our farm in Mississippi.

—Oprah Winfrey

The whole world opened to me when I learned to read.

—Mary McLeod Bethune

My grandfather went to school for one day: to tell the teacher he would not be back. Yet all of his adult life he read greedily, as did his uneducated friends.

—Toni Morrison

You think your pain and your heartbreak are unprecedented in the history of the world, but then you read. It was books that taught me that the things that tormented me most were the very things that connected me with all the people who were alive, or who had ever been alive.

—**James Baldwin**

When I read great literature, great drama, speeches, or sermons, I feel that the human mind has not achieved anything greater than the ability to share feelings and thoughts through language.

—**James Earl Jones**

I read to entertain myself, to educate myself, as a way to enlighten myself—as a way to challenge my beliefs about myself.

—**LeVar Burton**

It's the inspired student that continues to learn on their own. That's what separates the real achievers in the world from those who pedal along, finishing assignments.

—**Neil deGrasse Tyson**

Learning without wisdom is a load of books on a donkey's back.

—**Zora Neale Hurston,**
Moses, Man of the Mountain

The key to good decision making is not knowledge. It is understanding. We are swimming in the former. We are desperately lacking in the latter.

—**Malcolm Gladwell**

Nothing in all the world is more dangerous than sincere ignorance and conscientious stupidity.

—**Martin Luther King Jr.**

Armed with the knowledge of our past, we can with confidence charter a course for our future.

—**Malcolm X**

You may fill your heads with knowledge or skillfully train your hands, but unless it is based upon high, upright character, upon a true heart, it will amount to nothing.

—**Booker T. Washington**

The outside world told black kids when I was growing up that we weren't worth anything. But our parents said it wasn't so, and our churches and our schoolteachers said it wasn't so. They believed in us, and we, therefore, believed in ourselves.

—**Marian Wright Edelman**

Education is the key to unlock the golden door of freedom.

—**George Washington Carver**

Education and work are the levers to uplift a people. Education must not simply teach work—it must teach Life.

—**W. E. B. Du Bois**

Education is our passport to the future, for tomorrow belongs to the people who prepare for it today.

—**Malcolm X**

All of us must recognize that education and innovation will be the currency of the twenty-first century.

—**Barack Obama**

I'm not comfortable being preachy, but more people have to start spending as much time in the library as they do on the basketball court. If they took the idea that they could escape poverty through education, I think it would make a more basic and long-lasting change in the way things happen . . . What we need are positive, realistic goals and the willingness to work. Hard work and practical goals.

—**Kareem Abdul-Jabbar**

Sometimes folks ask us how we put up with racism and sexism to get our advanced college degrees. How could we stand it? Well, what choice did we have? What choice does anyone have? . . . If you are not educated—if you can't write clearly, speak articulately, think logically—you have lost control of your own life.

—**Sarah Louise Delany**

Education remains the key to both economic and political empowerment.

—**Barbara Jordan**

The question is not whether we can afford to invest in every child; it is whether we can afford not to.

—**Marian Wright Edelman**

Empower yourselves with a good education, then get out there and use that education to build a country worthy of your boundless promise.

—**Michelle Obama**

Education is the most powerful weapon which you can use to change the world.

—**Nelson Mandela**

Schooling is what happens inside the walls of the school, some of which is educational. Education happens everywhere, and it happens from the moment a child is born—and some people say before—until a person dies.

—Sara Lawrence-Lightfoot

As an educator, it's my duty to empower you to think. So that you can go forth and think accurate thoughts about how the world is put together.

—Neil deGrasse Tyson

What do we tell our children? Haste makes waste. Look before you leap. Stop and think. Don't judge a book by its cover. We believe that we are always better off gathering as much information as possible and spending as much time as possible in deliberation.

—Malcolm Gladwell

The questions which one asks oneself begin, at last, to illuminate the world, and become one's key to the experience of others.

—James Baldwin

Our whole life is but one great school; from the cradle to the grave we are all learners; nor will our education be finished until we die.

—Ann Plato

I had to make my own living and my own opportunity. But I made it! Don't sit down and wait for the opportunities to come. Get up and make them.

—**Madam C. J. Walker**

Fortunately, your generation has everything it takes to lead this country toward a brighter future. I'm confident that you can make the right choices—away from fear and division and paralysis, and toward cooperation and innovation and hope.

—**Barack Obama**

SLAVERY AND ITS LEGACY

From the day of its birth, the anomaly of slavery plagued a nation which asserted the equality of all men, and sought to derive powers of government from the consent of the governed. Within sound of the voices of those who said this lived more than half a million black slaves, forming nearly one-fifth of the population of a new nation.

—**W. E. B. Du Bois**

Rudely forced, they were, nevertheless, destined to help create a new world, to become the founding fathers and mothers of a new people.

—**Nathan Huggins**

For every hundred of us who survived the terrible journey across the Atlantic . . . four hundred of us perished. During three hundred years—the seventeenth, eighteenth, and nineteenth centuries—more than 100,000,000 of us were torn from our African homes.

—**Richard Wright**

The rule on the place was: Wake up the slaves at daylight, begin work when they can see, and quit work when they can't see.

—**Peter Clifton**

A tale of woe with tones loud, long, and deep; they breathed the prayers and complaints of souls boiling over with the bitterest anguish. Every tone was a testimony against slavery, and a prayer to God for deliverance from chains.

—Frederick Douglass

Slavery is terrible for men; but it is far more terrible for women. Super-added to the burdens common to all, they have wrongs and sufferings and mortifications peculiarly their own.

—Harriet Jacobs

For God's sake, don't be catch with pencil and paper. That was a major crime. You might as well had killed your marster or missus.

—Elijah Green

Our whole life is often a life of suffering. We cannot engage in business or dissipate ourselves in pleasure and riot as irreligious men too often do: We must bear our sorrows in silence, unknown and unpitied. We must often put on a face of serenity and cheerfulness when our hearts are torn with anguish or sinking in despair.

—Ann Plato

I don't see how we live, yet we is.

—Amy (Chavis) Perry

You never knew what it is to be a slave; to be entirely unprotected by law or custom; to have the laws reduce you to the condition of a chattel, entirely subject to the will of another. You never exhausted your ingenuity in avoiding the snares, and eluding the power of a hated tyrant; you never shuddered at the sound of his footsteps, and trembled within hearing of his voice.

—**Harriet Jacobs**

I could never be of any service to anyone as a slave.

—**Nat Turner**

Because God is not dead slavery can only end in blood.

—**Sojourner Truth**

The first excuse given to the civilized world for the murder of unoffending Negroes was the necessity of the white man to repress and stamp out "race riots." . . . It was always a remarkable feature in these insurrections and riots that only Negroes were killed during the rioting, and that all the white men escaped unharmed.

—**Ida B. Wells**

You have seen how a man was made a slave; you shall see how a slave was made a man.

—**Frederick Douglass**

Whenever and wherever men have been oppressed and enslaved, their oppressors and enslavers have, in every instance, found a warrant in the character of the victim.

—**Frederick Douglass**

When I found I had crossed that line [her first escape from slavery in 1845], I looked at my hands to see if I was the same person. There was such a glory over everything.

—**Harriet Tubman**

They can put him in a smoking car or baggage car—take him or leave him at a railroad station, exclude him from inns, drive him from all places of amusement or instruction without the least fear of the national government interfering for the protection of his liberty.

—**Frederick Douglass**

What, to the American slave, is your Fourth of July? I answer: A day that reveals to him, more than all other days in the year, the gross injustice and cruelty to which he is the constant victim. To him your celebration is a sham.

—**Frederick Douglass**

It has been a matter of deep interest to me to note the number of people who have come to shake hands with me after an address, who say that this is the first time they have ever called a Negro "Mister."

—**Booker T. Washington**

Lynching is the aftermath of slavery.

—**Mary Church Terrell**

The Black woman in the South who raises sons, grandsons, and nephews had her heartstrings tied to a hanging noose.

—**Maya Angelou**

Southern trees bear a strange fruit
Blood on the leaves and blood at the root
Black bodies swinging in the Southern breeze
Strange fruit hanging from the poplar trees.

—**Billie Holiday, "Strange Fruit"**

If we must die, let it not be like hogs
Hunted and penned in an inglorious spot.

—**Claude McKay, "If We Must Die"**

Only base men and oppressors can rejoice in a triumph of injustice over the weak and defenseless, for weakness ought itself to protect from assaults of pride, prejudice, and power.

—Frederick Douglass

We have been sentenced to die for something we ain't never done. Us poor boys been sentenced to burn up on the electric chair for the reason that we is workers—and the color of our skin is black.

—Andy and Leroy Wright, Olen Montgomery, Ozie Powell, Charlie Weems, Clarence Norris, Haywood Patterson, Eugene Williams, and Willie Roberson; collectively known as "The Scottsboro Boys"

But I don't know how to fight. All I know how to do is stay alive.

—Alice Walker, *The Color Purple*

The purpose of evil was to survive it.

—Toni Morrison, *Sula*

Separation is nothing but a form of slavery covered up with certain niceties of complexity.

—Martin Luther King Jr.

The very nature of segregation was demeaning, and its effect upon its victim was deadening.

—**Benjamin Davis Jr.**

I am not ashamed of my grandparents for having been slaves. I am only ashamed of myself for having at one time been ashamed.

—**Ralph Ellison**

It's going to take a lot of punching. Jim Crow won't be easy to stop. But I think there are enough thinking people in this fight, and enough ready to join to help bring real democracy to America.

—**Joe Louis**

I imagine one of the reasons people cling to their hates so stubbornly is because they sense, once hate is gone, they will be forced to deal with pain.

—**James Baldwin**

Oppression does not always crush the spirit of progress. Men will achieve in spite of it.

—**Carter G. Woodson**

I wake up every morning in a house that was built by slaves, and I watch my daughters—two beautiful, intelligent black young women—playing with their dogs on the White House lawn.

—**Michelle Obama**

Yes, African-Americans have felt the cold weight of shackles and the stinging lash of the field whip. But we've also dared to run north, and sing songs from Harriet Tubman's hymnal. We've buttoned up our Union Blues to join the fight for our freedom. We've railed against injustice for decade upon decade—a lifetime of struggle, and progress, and enlightenment that we see etched in Frederick Douglass's mighty, leonine gaze.

—**Barack Obama**

FREEDOM, RIGHTS, EQUALITY, AND JUSTICE

Injustice anywhere is a threat to justice everywhere.

—**Martin Luther King Jr.**

Freedom is a precious thing, and the inalienable birthright of all who travel this earth.

—**Paul Robeson**

There is no easy walk to freedom anywhere, and many of us will have to pass through the valley of the shadow of death again and again before we reach the mountaintop of our desires.

—**Nelson Mandela**

If there is no struggle, there is no progress. Those who profess to favor freedom, and yet deprecate agitation, are men who want crops without plowing up the ground, they want rain without thunder and lightning. They want the ocean without the awful roar of its many waters.

—**Frederick Douglass**

The cost of liberty is less than the price of repression.

—**W. E. B. Du Bois**

Freedom is never granted; it is won. Justice is never given; it is exacted.

—**A. Philip Randolph**

I am not truly free if I am taking away someone else's freedom, just as surely as I am not free when my freedom is taken away from me. The oppressed and the oppressor alike are robbed of their humanity.

—**Nelson Mandela**

Freedom is indivisible. Whites can't enjoy their separate freedoms. They spend too much time and resources defending those freedoms instead of enjoying them.

—**Desmond Tutu**

The only way to get equality is for two people to get the same thing at the same time at the same place.

—**Thurgood Marshall**

We know the road to freedom has always been stalked by death.

—**Angela Davis**

I had reasoned this out in my mind, there was two things I had a right to, liberty and death. If I could not have one, I would have the other, for no man should take me alive.

—**Harriet Tubman**

What does the Negro want? His answer is very simple. He wants only what all other Americans want. He wants opportunity to make real what the Declaration of Independence and the Constitution and the Bill of Rights say, what the Four Freedoms establish. While he knows these ideals are open to no man completely, he wants only his equal chance to obtain them.

—**Mary McLeod Bethune**

Human rights are God-given. Civil rights are man-made.

—**Adam Clayton Powell Jr.**

"We, the people." It is a very eloquent beginning. But when that document [the Preamble to the U.S. Constitution] was completed on the seventeenth of September in 1787 I was not included in that "We, the people." I felt somehow for many years that George Washington and Alexander Hamilton, just left me out by mistake. But through the process of amendment, interpretation, and court decision I have finally been included in "We, the people."

—**Barbara Jordan**

Words like "freedom," "justice," "democracy," are not common concepts; on the contrary, they are rare. People are not born knowing what these are. It takes enormous and, above all, individual effort to arrive at the respect for other people that these words imply.

—**James Baldwin**

My mother believed in freedom and equality even though we didn't know it for reality during our life in Alabama.

—**Rosa Parks**

The political core of any movement for freedom in the society has to have the political imperative to protect free speech.

—**bell hooks**

If the First Amendment means anything, it means that the State has no business telling a man, sitting alone in his own house, what books he may read or what films he may watch.

—**Thurgood Marshall**

To demand freedom is to demand justice. When there is no justice in the land, a man's freedom is threatened. Freedom and justice are interdependent. When a man has no protection under the law it is difficult for him to make others recognize him.

—**James Cone**

Once people begin to see the similarities between themselves and others, instead of focusing on differences, they come to recognize that equality is essentially a matter of human rights and human dignity.

—**John Lewis**

I won't "have it made" until the most underprivileged Negro in Mississippi can live in equal dignity with anyone else in America.

—**Jackie Robinson**

You learn about equality in history and civics, but you find out life is not really like that.

—**Arthur Ashe**

Struggle is a never-ending process. Freedom is never really won. You earn it and win it in every generation.

—**Coretta Scott King**

Where justice is denied, where poverty is enforced, where ignorance prevails, and where any one class is made to feel that society is in an organized conspiracy to oppress, rob, and degrade them, neither persons nor property will be safe.

—**Frederick Douglass**

A little girl grows up in Jim Crow Birmingham and she becomes the secretary of state.

—Condoleezza Rice

The only protection against injustice in man is power—physical, financial, and scientific.

—Marcus Garvey

It is certain, in any case, that ignorance, allied with power, is the most ferocious enemy justice can have.

—James Baldwin

I felt that one had better die fighting against injustice than to die like a dog or rat in a trap. I had already determined to sell my life as dearly as possible if attacked. I felt if I could take one lyncher with me, this would even up the score a little bit.

—Ida B. Wells

Efficiency can never be substituted for due process. Is not a dictatorship the more "efficient" form of government?

—Thurgood Marshall

If one really wishes to know how justice is administered in a country, one does not question the policemen, the lawyers, the judges, or the protected members of the middle class. One goes to the unprotected—those, precisely, who need the law's protection most!—and listens to their testimony.

—**James Baldwin**

I'll tell you who is the greatest agitator in this country . . . the greatest agitator is injustice.

—**William Pickens**

We call on America to sow the seeds of social justice and racial equality that it may reap a harvest of righteousness and freedom for all.

—**John E. Jacob**

Social change rarely comes about through the efforts of the disenfranchised. The middle class creates social revolutions. When a group of people are disproportionately concerned with daily survival, it's not likely that they have the resources to go to Washington and march.

—**Faye Wattleton**

23

Charity is no substitute for justice withheld.

—St. Augustine

Human progress is neither automatic nor inevitable . . . Every step toward the goal of justice requires sacrifice, suffering, and struggle; the tireless exertions and passionate concern of dedicated individuals.

—Martin Luther King Jr.

If you are neutral in situations of injustice, you have chosen the side of the oppressor. If an elephant has its foot on the tail of a mouse, and you say that you are neutral, the mouse will not appreciate your neutrality.

—Desmond Tutu

I see that the path of progress has never taken a straight line, but has always been a zigzag course amid the conflicting forces of right and wrong, truth and error, justice and injustice, cruelty and mercy.

—Kelly Miller

Laws not only provide concrete benefits; they can even change the hearts of men—some men anyway—for good or evil. . . . The hearts of men do not change of themselves.

—Thurgood Marshall

Well, charity ain't justice. Charity is beautiful, but you ain't got to be charitable to me if I already got justice. If I already got a sense of participation, you ain't got to be charitable to me. Just treat me right every day.

—**Michael Eric Dyson**

Let there be justice for all. Let there be peace for all. Let there be work, bread, water and salt for all. Let each know that for each the body, the mind and the soul have been freed to fulfill themselves.

—**Nelson Mandela**

RACE AND RACISM

To talk about race in America is to explore the wilderness inside ourselves and to come to terms with a history that we'd rather conceal.

—Cornel West

The relation subsisting between the white and colored people of this country is the great, paramount, imperative, and all-commanding question for this age and nation to solve.

—Frederick Douglass

I am not tragically colored. There is no great sorrow dammed up in my soul, nor lurking behind my eyes. . . . Even in the helter-skelter skirmish that is my life, I have seen that the world is to the strong regardless of a little pigmentation more or less. No, I do not weep at the world—I am too busy sharpening my oyster knife.

—Zora Neale Hurston

All of us are black first, and everything else second.

—Malcolm X

I am an invisible man. . . . I am a man of substance, of flesh and bone, fiber and liquids—and I might even be said to possess a mind. I am invisible, understand, simply because people refuse to see me.

—**Ralph Ellison,** *Invisible Man*

Goddammit, look! We live here and they live there. We black and they white. They got things and we ain't. They do things and we can't. It's just like living in jail.

—**Richard Wright,** *Native Son*

Being black is the greatest burden I've had to bear.

—**Arthur Ashe**

The children of these disillusioned colored pioneers inherited the total lot of their parents—the disappointments, the anger. To add to their misery, they had little hope of deliverance. For where does one run to when he's already in the promised land?

—**Claude Brown**

It is the duty of the younger Negro artist . . . to change through the force of his art that old whispering "I want to be white," hidden in the aspirations of his people, to "Why should I want to be white? I am a Negro—and beautiful!"

—**Langston Hughes**

I have found no better way of avoiding race prejudice than to act with people of other races as if prejudice did not exist.

—Jack Johnson

The fact that white people readily and proudly call themselves "white," glorify all that is white, and whitewash all that is glorified, becomes unnatural and bigoted in its intent only when these same whites deny persons of African heritage who are Black the natural and inalienable right to readily—proudly—call themselves "black," glorify all that is black, and blackwash all that is glorified.

—Abbey Lincoln

A little black girl yearns for the blue eyes of a little white girl, and the horror at the heart of her yearning is exceeded only by the evil of fulfillment.

—Toni Morrison, *The Bluest Eye*

In all the relations of life and death, we are met by the color line.

—Frederick Douglass

A greater truth that I think we are faced with on a day-to-day basis as minorities is: We are the color of skin first and people second.

—Jordan Peele

Not that I'd want to forget being black, but I would love to walk through life without the anxiety of being prejudged and pigeonholed on the basis of my race.

—**Rita Dove**

Sometimes, I feel discriminated against, but it does not make me angry. It merely astonishes me. How can any deny themselves the pleasure of my company?

—**Zora Neale Hurston**

Racism is a contempt for life, an arrogant assertion that one race is the center of value and object of devotion, before which other races must kneel in submission.

—**Martin Luther King Jr.**

Racism keeps people who are being managed from finding out the truth through contact with each other.

—**Shirley Chisholm**

I am a person who has never completely escaped from the scars of my childhood. Racism, which leaves a shadow on one's sense of accomplishment, can make one feel like a perpetual outsider.

—**Alvin Ailey**

Racism is a scholarly pursuit. . . . [it] is taught, institutionalized.

—**Toni Morrison**

I think if you're an interracial child and you're strong enough to live "I'm neither black nor white but in the middle," then, more power. But I needed to make a choice and feel part of this culture. I feel a lot of pride in being a black woman.

—**Halle Berry**

I recall my mother telling me that just because you are black, you are going to have to work 100 percent more than everyone else just to be considered equal. That is unfair, but it is the reality of the situation.

—**Vanessa Williams**

I never doubted my ability, but when you hear all your life you're inferior, it makes you wonder if the other guys have something you've never seen before. If they do, I'm still looking for it.

—**Hank Aaron**

I've always maintained that black people and women suffer from a presumption of incompetence. The burdens of proof are different. It just gets so tiresome.

—**Carol Moseley Braun**

For racism to die, a totally different America must be born.

—Stokely Carmichael

Racism is so universal in this country, so widespread and deep-seated, that it is invisible because it is so normal.

—Shirley Chisholm

As long as you keep a person down, some part of you has to be down there to hold him down, so it means you cannot soar as you otherwise might.

—Marian Anderson

I think for a number of people, the idea of a secure, confident male who is black is disturbing, and possibly unnerving.

—Bryant Gumbel

I've learned that I must find positive outlets for anger or it will destroy me. There is a certain anger: it reaches such intensity that to express it fully would require homicidal rage—self-destructive, destroy-the-world rage—and its flame burns because the world is so unjust. I have to try to find a way to channel that anger to the positive, and the highest positive is forgiveness.

—Sidney Poitier

Racism is a moral catastrophe, most graphically seen in the prison industrial complex and targeted police surveillance in black and brown ghettos rendered invisible in public discourse.

—Cornel West

Walking around as a black man in America, I have more worry about the police than the KKK.

—W. Kamau Bell

If I weren't earning more than $3 million a year to dunk a basketball, most people on the street would run in the other direction if they saw me coming.

—Charles Barkley

Black people have never had the power to enforce racism, and so this is something that white America is going to have to work out themselves. If they decide they want to stop it, curtail it, or do the right thing . . . then it will be done, but not until then.

—Spike Lee

I just think racism is within each and every one of us. It's everyone's responsibility to figure out how they deal with this kind of obsolete instinct.

—Jordan Peele

African Americans have come too far and we have too far yet to go to take a detour into the swamp of hatred . . . . Never let the dying hand of racism rest on your shoulder, weighing you down. Let racism always be someone else's burden to carry.

—Colin Powell

Challenging racism means putting committed people in place before the fact, and empowering them to make decisions based on the principle that we all deserve to be treated with basic human dignity.

—Solomon Jones

Americans believe in the reality of "race" as a defined, indubitable feature of the natural world. Racism—the need to ascribe bone-deep features to people and then humiliate, reduce, and destroy them—inevitably follows from this inalterable condition. In this way, racism is rendered as the innocent daughter of Mother Nature, and one is left to deplore the Middle Passage or Trail of Tears the way one deplores an earthquake, a tornado, or any other phenomenon that can be cast as beyond the handiwork of men. But race is the child of racism, not the father.

—Ta-Nehisi Coates

I have asserted a firm conviction—a conviction rooted in my faith in God and my faith in the American people—that working together we can move beyond some of our old racial wounds, and that in fact we have no choice if we are to continue on the path of a more perfect union.

—Barack Obama

THE CIVIL RIGHTS MOVEMENT

We cannot stand still; we cannot permit ourselves simply to be victims.

—W. E. B. Du Bois

We are here to serve notice that we are in a fight to the death for the rights guaranteed us as American citizens by the Constitution.

—James Weldon Johnson

We didn't have any of what they called Civil Rights back then. It was just a matter of survival—existing from day to day.

—Rosa Parks

The Negro himself will more readily acquiesce in his lot unless he has a legally recognized claim to a better life. I think the segregation decision of 1954 probably did more than anything else to awaken the Negro from his apathy to demanding his right to equality.

—Thurgood Marshall

I could see that my significance as an individual was small in this affair. I had become, whether I liked it or not, a symbol representing my people.

—**Marian Anderson**

History will have to record that the greatest tragedy of this period of social transition was not the strident clamor of the bad people, but the appalling silence of the good people.

—**Martin Luther King Jr.**

At the rate things are going here, all of Africa will be free before we can get a lousy cup of coffee.

—**James Baldwin**

We are not fighting for integration, nor are we fighting for separation. We are fighting for recognition as human beings. We are fighting for . . . human rights.

—**Malcolm X**

While I had been fighting in Vietnam alongside brave soldiers trying to preserve their freedom, in my own land a long-simmering conflict had turned into an open fight in our streets and cities—a fight that had to be won.

—**Colin Powell**

I have a dream that one day on the red hills of Georgia the sons of former slaves and the sons of former slaveowners will be able to sit down together at the table of brotherhood.

—**Martin Luther King Jr.**

When you talk about black power you talk about bringing this country to its knees any time it messes with the black man.

—**Stokely Carmichael**

The day that the black man takes an uncompromising step and realizes that he's within his rights, when his own freedom is being jeopardized, to use any means necessary to bring about his freedom or put a halt to that injustice, I don't think he'll be by himself.

—**Malcolm X**

I'm not concerned with your liking or disliking me. All I ask is that you respect me as a human being.

—**Jackie Robinson**

What hurt me most about the glorious black awakening of the late sixties and early seventies is that we lost our sense of humor. Many of us thought that enlightened politics excluded it.

—**Henry Louis Gates Jr.**

Nonviolence is the answer to the crucial political and moral questions of our time; the need for man to overcome oppression and violence without resorting to oppression and violence. Man must evolve for all human conflict a method which rejects revenge, aggression and retaliation. The foundation of such a method is love.

—**Martin Luther King Jr.**

I had no idea when I refused to give up my seat on that Montgomery bus that my small action would help put an end to the segregation laws in the South. I only knew that I was tired of being pushed around. I was a regular person, just as good as anybody else. There had been a few times in my life when I was treated by white people like a regular person, so I knew what that felt like. It was time. It was time that other white people started treating me that way.

—**Rosa Parks**

Sammy Davis Jr., Duke Ellington, Count Basie, Lena Horne, Sidney Poitier—we weren't leading the charge. We weren't at the forefront, getting our heads cracked open, though our careers were a reflection of what was possible when attention was paid. Twenty-five years earlier it hadn't been widely expected, with opportunities so meager, that blacks could be scientists, statesmen, artists. Every time I stepped out, I felt the responsibility to do whatever I could to make pending successes seem a natural expectation.

—**Sidney Poitier**

I've been marching since I was seventeen, long before there was a Civil Rights Movement. I was marching through the lobby of the Waldorf-Astoria, of the Sands . . . to a table at the Copa. And I marched alone. Worse. Often to Black derision.

—Sammy Davis Jr.

I am a candidate for the Presidency of the United States. I make that statement proudly, in the full knowledge that, as a black person and as a female person, I do not have a chance of actually gaining that office in this election year.

—Shirley Chisholm

It must be remembered that during most of the past 200 years the Constitution as interpreted by this Court did not prohibit the most ingenious and pervasive forms of discrimination against the Negro. Now, when a state acts to remedy the effects of that legacy of discrimination, I cannot believe that this same Constitution stands as a barrier. At every point from birth to death the impact of the past is reflected in the still disfavored position of the Negro. In light of the sorry history of discrimination and its devastating impact on the lives of Negroes, bringing the Negro into the mainstream of American life should be a state interest of the highest order.

—Thurgood Marshall

You're either part of the solution or part of the problem.

—Eldridge Cleaver

Malcolm is gone and Martin is gone, and it is up to all of us to nourish the hope they gave us.

—Lena Horne

The very class that owes its new affluence to the Movement now refuses to support the organizations that made its success possible, and has retreated from its concern for black people who are poor.

—Alice Walker

My right and my privilege to stand here before you has been won— won in my lifetime—by the blood and the sweat of the innocent.

—Jesse Jackson

A majority of this Court signals that it regards racial discrimination as largely a phenomenon of the past, and that government bodies need no longer preoccupy themselves with rectifying racial injustice . . . I, however, do not believe this nation is anywhere close to eradicating racial discrimination or its vestiges.

—Thurgood Marshall

But we believed if we kept on working, if we kept on marching, if we kept on voting, if we kept on believing, we would make America beautiful for everybody.

—Al Sharpton

I stand before you today as the elected leader of the greatest city of a great nation, to which my ancestors were brought, chained and whipped in the hold of a slave ship. We have not finished the journey toward liberty and justice, but surely we have come a long way.

—**David Dinkins**

In one generation we have moved from denying a black man service at a lunch counter to elevating one to the highest military office in the nation, and to being a serious contender for the presidency. This is a magnificent country and I am proud to be one of its sons.

—**Colin Powell**

Sometimes I hear people saying nothing has changed, but for someone to grow up the way I grew up in the cotton fields of Alabama to now be serving in the United States Congress makes me want to tell them come and walk in my shoes. Come walk in the shoes of those who were attacked by police dogs, fire hoses and nightsticks, arrested, and taken to jail.

—**John Lewis**

Because of the Civil Rights movement, new doors of opportunity and education swung open for everybody . . . Not just for blacks and whites, but also women and Latinos; and Asians and Native Americans; and gay Americans and Americans with a disability. They swung open for you, and they swung open for me. And that's why I'm standing here today—because of those efforts, because of that legacy.

—**Barack Obama**

GOVERNMENT, DEMOCRACY, AND ACTIVISM

The day will come when Americans will realize that a government that will not protect its citizens cannot demand protection for itself.

—*Black Chronicle*, June 1, 1896

I asked, "Where is the black man's Government" . . . . "Where is his President, his country, and his ambassador, his army, his navy, his men of big affairs?" I could not find them, and then I declared, "I will help to make them."

—**Marcus Garvey**

No government has the right to hide behind national sovereignty in order to violate the human rights or fundamental freedoms of its peoples.

—**Kofi Annan**

In the end, if the people cannot trust their government to do the job for which it exists—to protect them and to promote their common welfare—all else is lost.

—**Barack Obama**

This country can have no more democracy than it accords and guarantees to the humblest and weakest citizen.

—**James Weldon Johnson**

After all, democracy takes place when the silenced find a voice, and when we begin to listen to what they have to say.

—**Lani Guinier**

Of course, the aim of a constitutional democracy is to safeguard the rights of the minority and avoid the tyranny of the majority.

—**Cornel West**

People often don't realize how fragile democracy is until it breaks.

—**DeRay Mckesson**

A government of, by, and for the people requires that people talk to people, that we can agree to disagree but do so in civility. If we let the politicians and those who report dictate our discourse, then our course will be dictated.

—**Donna Brazile**

The obstacles to democracy have little to do with culture or religion, and much more to do with the desire of those in power to maintain their position at any cost.

—**Kofi Annan**

The strongest democracies flourish from frequent and lively debate, but they endure when people of every background and belief find a way to set aside smaller differences in service of a greater purpose.

—**Barack Obama**

Thus shall we live, because we will have created a society which recognizes that all people are born equal, with each entitled in equal measure to life, liberty, prosperity, human rights and good governance.

—**Nelson Mandela**

A functioning, robust democracy requires a healthy, educated, participatory followership and an educated, morally grounded leadership.

—**Chinua Achebe**

Where you see wrong or inequality or injustice, speak out, because this is your country. This is your democracy. Make it. Protect it. Pass it on.

—**Thurgood Marshall**

As long as poverty, injustice, and gross inequality exist in our world, none of us can truly rest.

—**Nelson Mandela**

I cannot imagine how knowing one's history would not urge one to be an activist.

—**John Hope Franklin**

Until the killing of black men, black mothers' sons, becomes as important to the rest of the country as the killing of a white mother's son, we who believe in freedom cannot rest.

—**Ella Baker**

You have a duty in this moment in history to take action and stand on the side of people who have been oppressed for generations.

—**Opal Tometi**

I am not looking for approval. I have to stand up for people that are oppressed. If they take football away, my endorsements from me, I know that I stood up for what is right.

—**Colin Kaepernick**

It's about being bold and creative and innovative so that new opportunities are unlocked along the way, and we don't have to keep banging our heads against a wall trying to solve the same old problem. I don't want to keep having this debate about whether or not black lives matter. I want to solve different kinds of problems. And so that's how I focus and prioritize: I want to work on things that get us closer to that.

—**Alicia Garza**

These movements aren't about anger. We're not angrily saying "Black Lives Matter." We're declaring it. It's a declaration. We want to be seen as robust, full human beings that have anger and have joy. We want to be able to just freely have that joy. Like everybody else does.

—**Tarana Burke**

How many more mothers? How many more fathers need to shed tears of grief before we do something? Give us a vote. Let us vote. We came here to do our job. We came here to work.

—**John Lewis, demanding common-sense gun control legislation**

Nonviolent protest is important and has always been to advancing our nation. From Muhammad Ali to artists and entertainers who participated in movements, from the women's rights movement to the civil rights movement, this is a noble tradition in our country.

—**Cory Booker**

People seeking common-sense gun control must become single-issue voters on gun control. Support for more restrictions may not be the only reason to vote for a candidate, but it must be sufficient to vote against one. We have to stop waiting for politicians to display courage and instead start to instill fear in them.

—**Charles M. Blow**

I understand the Second Amendment. I respect the Second Amendment. I think we need to use common-sense tools to keep the American people safe, to keep our streets safe.

—**Eric Holder**

I don't know one woman who hasn't been sexually harassed. Men just don't get it. It's an economic issue for women . . . It has to do with equality in the workplace.

—**Carol Moseley Braun**

If I can symbolize the ability to pursue gender equality, racial equality, and to be truthful about our experiences, then, absolutely, that's what I want to be.

—**Anita Hill**

The struggle is eternal. Somebody else carries on.

—**Ella Baker**

#MeToo is essentially about survivors supporting survivors. And it's really about community healing and community action. Although we can't define what healing looks like for people, we can set the stage and give people the resources to have access to healing. And that means legitimate things like policies and laws that change that support survivors.

—**Tarana Burke**

Today there are people trying to take away rights that our mothers, grandmothers, and great-grandmothers fought for: our right to vote, our right to choose, affordable quality education, equal pay, access to health care. We the people can't let that happen.

—**Kerry Washington**

It's easy to feel overwhelmed by the challenges we face. But progress does not happen overnight. It may be painful and even slow at times, but we cannot throw up our hands at the first—or even fifth—setback. We must roll up our sleeves, knock on doors and register people to vote.

—**Kamala Harris**

Do not look the other way; do not hesitate. Recognize that the world is hungry for action, not words. Act with courage and vision.

—**Nelson Mandela**

AMERICA

We black folk, our history and our present being, are a mirror of all the manifold experiences of America. What we want, what we represent, what we endure is what America is. If we black folk perish, America will perish.

—Richard Wright

Your country? How came it yours?

—W. E. B. Du Bois

The patriots of 1776 did not fight to replace the tyranny of a king with the privileges of a few or the rule of a mob. They gave to us a republic, a government of, and by, and for the people, entrusting each generation to keep safe our founding creed. And for more than two hundred years, we have.

—Barack Obama

I have confidence not only in my country and her institutions but in the endurance, capacity and destiny of my people.

—Blanche K. Bruce

The destiny of the colored American . . . is the destiny of America.

—Frederick Douglass

My father was a slave, and my people died to build this country, and I'm going to stay right here, and have a part of it just like you. And no fascist-minded people will drive me from it. Is that clear?

—Paul Robeson, testimony before the House Committee on Un-American Activities, June 12, 1956

We have to undo the millions of little white lies that America told itself and the world about the American Black man.

—John O. Killens

Our children, our jobless men, our deprived, rejected, and starving fellow citizens must come first. For this reason, I intend to vote No on every money bill that comes to the floor of this House that provides any funds for the Department of Defense.

—Shirley Chisholm

I am America. Only, I'm the part you won't recognize. But get used to me. Black, confident, cocky; my name, not yours; my religion, not yours; my goals, my own—get used to me!

—Muhammad Ali

The meaning of America is the possibilities of the common man. It is a refutation of that widespread assumption that the real makers of the world must always be a small group of exceptional men, while most men are incapable of assisting civilization or achieving culture. The United States of America proves, if it proves anything, that the number of men who may be educated and may achieve is much larger than the world has hitherto assumed.

—W. E. B. Du Bois

America is me. It gave me the only life I know, so I must share in its survival.

—Gordon Parks

If we had been allowed to participate in the vital processes of America's national growth, what would have been the textures of our lives, the pattern of our traditions, the routine of our customs, the state of our arts, the code of our laws, the function of our government! . . . We black folk say that America would have been stronger and greater.

—Richard Wright

It is utterly exhausting being Black in America—physically, mentally, and emotionally. While many minority groups and women feel similar stress, there is no respite or escape from your badge of color.

—Marian Wright Edelman

Our nation is a rainbow—red, yellow, brown, black, and white—and we're all precious in God's sight.

—Jesse Jackson

At no point in my life have I ever felt as though I were an American.

—Toni Morrison

I love America more than any other country in the world, and, exactly for this reason, I insist on the right to criticize her perpetually.

—James Baldwin

A lesser people—I mean a people of weaker constitution and fortitude—would have given up on this country long ago. But we didn't. We are going to force this country to live up to what it is supposed to be about or we'll die in the attempt.

—Barbara Jordan

America is a living idea. It isn't only the tenets of its founding, but also the terms of its future. Every day, we make America. Seeking to preserve and enshrine one vision of this country from one period of its past robs it of what makes it magical: its infinite possibility for adjustment.

—Charles M. Blow

I am particularly struck by the number of aged men who represent America. It seems we are not taking into consideration what is happening in this country today. We are not giving bright young people—who are often so much in touch with the time—a sufficient chance to break into politics and be heard.

—**Shirley Chisholm**

America is essentially a dream, a dream as yet unfulfilled. It is a dream of a land where men of all races, of all nationalities, and of all creeds can live together as brothers.

—**Martin Luther King Jr.**

I am the American Dream. I am the epitome of what the American Dream basically said. It said you could come from anywhere and be anything you want in this country. That's exactly what I've done.

—**Whoopi Goldberg**

Hope is what led me here today—with a father from Kenya, a mother from Kansas; and a story that could only happen in the United States of America. Hope is the bedrock of this nation; the belief that our destiny will not be written for us, but by us; by all those men and women who are not content to settle for the world as it is; who have courage to remake the world as it should be.

—**Barack Obama**

I am not fighting just for myself and my people in the South when I fight for freedom and equality. I realize now that I fight for the moral and political health of America as a whole and for her position in the world at large.

—**Marian Wright Edelman**

America was a thing I saw on TV—that wasn't a real world. That wasn't within my realm of dreaming.

—**Trevor Noah**

The American dream belongs to all of us.

—**Kamala Harris**

What I really feel is necessary is that the black people in this country will have to upset this apple cart. We can no longer ignore the fact that America is *not* the . . . land of the free and the home of the brave.

—**Fannie Lou Hamer**

We have drained common sense out of our politics. The more we focus on tactics and games, the more good people check out and give up.

—**Deval Patrick**

That's the America I know. That's the country we love. Clear-eyed. Big-hearted. Undaunted by challenge. Optimistic that unarmed truth and unconditional love will have the final word. That's what makes me so hopeful about our future. I believe in change because I believe in you, the American people.

—**Barack Obama**

The life of the nation is secure only while the nation is honest, truthful, and virtuous.

—**Frederick Douglass**

My fellow Americans, we cannot be seduced into cynicism about our politics, because cynicism is a refuge for cowards and this nation is and must always be the home of the brave. We are the United States of America. We will not falter or fail. We will not retreat or surrender— we will not surrender our values, we will not surrender our ideals, we will not surrender the moral high ground.

—**Cory Booker**

LOVE AND KINDNESS

Love is the most durable power in the world. This creative force is the most potent instrument available in mankind's quest for peace and security.

—**Martin Luther King Jr.**

Love has no awareness of merit or demerit; it has no scale by which its portion may be weighed or measured. It does not seek to balance giving and receiving. Love loves; this is its nature.

—**Howard Thurman**

Love, I find is like singing. Everybody can do enough to satisfy themselves, though it may not impress the neighbors as being very much.

—**Zora Neale Hurston**

The workings of the human heart are the profoundest mystery of the universe. One moment they make us despair of our kind, and the next we see in them the reflection of the divine image.

—**Charles W. Chesnutt**

To love is to make of one's heart a swinging door.

—Howard Thurman

Love without esteem cannot go far or reach high. It is an angel with only one wing.

—Alexandre Dumas

I'm not done with love, but I refuse to settle. I am a hopeless romantic. And I won't stop till I get it right.

—Halle Berry

If your love for me requires that I hide parts of who I am, then you don't love me. Love is never a request for silence.

—DeRay Mckesson

Now me, when I want ready-made trouble, I dig up a handsome man.

—Gloria Naylor, *The Women of Brewster Place*

A lost love is like a toothache. It'll hurt you and it'll hurt so much you'll finally get rid of it. You'll miss it but you'll feel better.

—Duke Ellington

Love does not begin and end the way we seem to think it does.
Love is a battle, love is a war; love is growing up.

—**James Baldwin**

I love who I am, and I encourage other people to love and embrace
who they are. But it definitely wasn't easy—it took me a while.

—**Serena Williams**

Sometimes, when we're lying together, I look at her and I feel dizzy
with the realization that here is another distinct person from me, who
has memories, origins, thoughts, feelings that are different from my
own. That tension between familiarity and mystery meshes something
strong between us. Even if one builds a life together based on trust,
attentiveness, and mutual support, I think that it's important that a
partner continues to surprise.

—**Barack Obama**

Your ordinary acts of love and hope point to the extraordinary promise
that every human life is of inestimable value.

—**Desmond Tutu**

There is always something left to love. And if you ain't learned that,
you ain't learning nothing.

—**Lorraine Hansberry, *A Raisin in the Sun***

My parents never wanted me to get too heady. Gratitude was to be my gravity, so they never stopped reminding me that my blessings sprang from countless ordinary Americans who had shown extraordinary acts of kindness and decency; people who struggled, sweat, and bled for our rights, people who fought and paid the ultimate price for the freedoms we enjoy. I was told that we can't pay those Americans back for their colossal acts of service, but we have an obligation to pay it forward to others through our service and sacrifice.

—**Cory Booker**

Service is the rent we pay for living. It is the very purpose of life and not something you do in your spare time.

—**Marian Wright Edelman**

If we love a child, and the child senses that we love him, he will get a concept of love that all subsequent hatred in the world will never be able to destroy.

—**Howard Thurman**

The moment we choose to love we begin to move against domination, against oppression. The moment we choose to love we begin to move towards freedom, to act in ways that liberate ourselves and others.

—**bell hooks**

When you are kind to someone in trouble, you hope they'll remember and be kind to someone else. And it'll become like a wildfire.

—**Whoopi Goldberg**

There is always something to do. There are hungry people to feed, naked people to clothe, sick people to comfort and make well. And while I don't expect you to save the world I do think it's not asking too much for you to love those with whom you sleep, share the happiness of those whom you call friend, engage those among you who are visionary and remove from your life those who offer you depression, despair and disrespect.

—**Nikki Giovanni**

I leave you love. Love builds. It is positive and helpful. It is more beneficial than hate. Injuries quickly forgotten quickly pass away. Personally and racially, our enemies must be forgiven. . . .

—**Mary McLeod Bethune**

I have decided to stick with love . . . Hate is too great a burden to bear.

—**Martin Luther King Jr.**

Life is just a short walk from the cradle to the grave—and it sure behooves us to be kind to one another along the way.

—**Alice Childress**

How far you go in life depends on your being tender with the young, compassionate with the aged, sympathetic with the striving, and tolerant of the weak and strong. Because someday in your life you will have been all of these.

—George Washington Carver

No one is born hating another person because of the color of his skin, or his background, or his religion. People must learn to hate, and if they can learn to hate, they can be taught to love, for love comes more natural to the human heart than its opposite.

—Nelson Mandela

FAMILY AND FRIENDSHIP

Of all the rocks upon which we build our lives, we are reminded today that family is the most important.

—Barack Obama

Mama exhorted her children at every opportunity to "jump at de sun." We might not land on the sun, but at least we would get off the ground.

—Zora Neale Hurston, *Dust Tracks on a Road*

My mom raised me as if there were no limitations on where I could go or what I could do. When I look back I realize she raised me like a white kid—not white culturally, but in the sense of believing that the world was my oyster, that I should speak up for myself, that my ideas and thoughts and decisions mattered.

—Trevor Noah

What I most remember was an abiding sense of comfort and security. I got plenty of mothering not only from Pop and my brothers and sisters when they were home, but from the whole of our close-knit community.

—Paul Robeson

I do not recollect of ever seeing my mother by the light of day. She would lie down with me and get me to sleep, but long before I waked she was gone.

—**Frederick Douglass**

To describe my mother would be to write about a hurricane in its perfect power.

—**Maya Angelou**

My mom was the most fantastic woman in the world. She only went to the fifth grade, but she knew there was nothing wrong with my brain, I just couldn't see.

—**Ray Charles**

I had a series of childhood illnesses. It started off as scarlet fever, and from there it was polio. My father was the one who sort of babied me and was sympathetic. . . . My mother was the one who made me work, made me believe that one day it would be possible for me to walk without braces.

—**Wilma Rudolph**

My mother never gave up on me. I messed up in school so much they were sending me home, but my mother sent me right back.

—**Denzel Washington**

Even today, when I think about my mother for any reason, what first jumps to mind are memories of her telling me that she loved me more than anyone else in the world.

—**Bill Russell**

You made us believe, you kept us off the street. You put clothes on our backs, food on the table. When you didn't eat, you made sure we ate. You went to sleep hungry. You sacrificed for us. You're the real MVP.

—**Kevin Durant**

My mom always taught us that family's all you have when everything's said and done. You have to love them and support them no matter who they are, no matter how they look, no matter how they behave.

—**Toni Braxton**

For I am my mother's daughter, and the drums of Africa still beat in my heart. They will not let me rest while there is a single Negro boy or girl without a chance to prove his worth.

—**Mary McLeod Bethune**

I know that she was the kindest, most generous spirit I have ever known, and that what is best in me I owe to her.

—**Barack Obama**

My mother was and will always remain my greatest hero.

—**Kamala Harris**

Fatherhood is responsibility, it's definitely humility, a lot of love, and the friendship of a parent and child.

—**Denzel Washington**

I felt something impossible for me to explain in words. Then when they took her away, it hit me. I got scared all over again and began to feel giddy. Then it came to me—I was a father.

—**Nat "King" Cole**

Being a dad is about setting your priorities in the right place, listening to your partner and paying attention to what they might need. It's not letting work or outside distractions take away from those moments. You can read all the books you want and get all the advice you want, but the key is doing it with intention and mindfulness.

—**John Legend**

From the first time the doctor placed you in my arms I knew I'd meet death before I'd let you meet harm. Although questions arose in my mind, would I be man enough?

—**Will Smith**

The measure of a man is how well he provides for his children.

—Sidney Poitier

I find myself looking at my children, just watching them and realizing how fortunate I am. Everything I've done on the basketball court, in business, nothing compares to having them.

—Michael Jordan

He was my first teacher in public speaking, and long before my days as a class orator and college debater there were the evenings or recitations at home, where his love for the eloquent and meaningful word and his insistence on purity of diction made their impress.

—Paul Robeson

My father was a feminist from the day I was born; there was nothing his little girl couldn't do. And he modeled that in his relationship with my mother.

—Condoleezza Rice

My earliest memories of my father are of seeing him work at his desk and realizing that he was happy. I did not know it then, but that was one of the most precious gifts a father can give his child.

—Malcolm Gladwell

In African-American culture, the least discussed thing amongst men is the fact that they really wish they had fathers. There's a lot of single black women who did the best that they could and that's a beautiful thing, but they don't know how necessary a father is in a kid's life and how much guys miss that deep down inside. That's why they gravitate towards gangs. That's why they gravitate toward older guys who may lead them in a negative direction, because they just want to be embraced by a man.

—LL Cool J

My dad was such a good dad that when he left, he left a huge scar. He was my superhero.

—Jay-Z

Black people love their children with a kind of obsession. You are all we have, and you come to us endangered. I think we would like to kill you ourselves before seeing you killed by the streets that America made. That is a philosophy of the disembodied, of a people who control nothing, who can protect nothing. . . .

—Ta-Nehisi Coates

I was raised in a sort of village. I have a huge family, and I think there is strength in that. It helped me to deal with some of the complications of living in the South because I always felt like I belonged, no matter what.

—Chadwick Boseman

We learned about dignity and decency—that how hard you work matters more than how much you make . . . . That helping others means more than just getting ahead yourself.

—**Michelle Obama**

Feeling secure in your worth often stems from knowing you belong to two very special groups—your family and your community.

—**Dorothy S. Strickland**

A child must have a sense of selfhood, a knowledge that he is not here by sufferance, that his forbears contributed to the country and to the world.

—**John O. Killens**

Some people are your relatives but others are your ancestors, and you choose the ones you want to have as ancestors. You create yourself out of those values.

—**Ralph Ellison**

Children—all children—are the world. Children are hope and life. Children are our immortality. Children are the seeds and the molders of history and the transmitters of our values—good and bad.

—**Marian Wright Edelman**

There's only one thing we can be sure of, and that is the love that we have—for our children, for our families, for each other. The warmth of a small child's embrace—that is true. The memories we have of them, the joy that they bring, the wonder we see through their eyes, that fierce and boundless love we feel for them, a love that takes us out of ourselves, and binds us to something larger—we know that's what matters.

—**Barack Obama**

I have come to realize that what distinguishes one child from another is not ability, but access. Access to education, access to opportunity, access to love.

—**Lauryn Hill**

To be a mother to a child is the most brilliant gift; it's gorgeous.

—**Alicia Keys**

Being a friend means mastering the art of timing. There is a time for silence. A time to let go and allow people to hurl themselves into their own destiny. And a time to pick up the pieces when it's all over.

—**Octavia E. Butler**

I love my husband, but it is nothing like a conversation with a woman that understands you.

—**Beyoncé Knowles-Carter**

No person is your friend (or kin) who demands your silence, or denies your right to grow and be perceived as fully blossomed as you were intended.

—**Alice Walker**

Hold a true friend with both hands.

—**African Proverb**

WORK, ARTISTRY, AND SUCCESS

The return from your work must be the satisfaction which that work brings you and the world's need of that work. With this, life is heaven, or as near heaven as you can get. Without this—with work which you despise, which bores you, and which the world does not need—this life is hell.

—W. E. B. Du Bois

All work is honorable. Always do your best because someone is watching.

—Colin Powell

I had to succeed. I would never stop trying, never. A violinist had his violin, a painter his palette. All I had was myself. I was the instrument that I must care for.

—Josephine Baker

Man, if you gotta ask you'll never know.

—Louis Armstrong, about the meaning of jazz

All art is a kind of confession, more or less oblique. All artists, if they are to survive, are forced, at last, to tell the whole story, to vomit the anguish up.

—**James Baldwin**

Through their untarnishable beauty, they seem assured of the immortality of those great folk expressions that survive not so much through being typical of a group or representative of a period as by virtue of being fundamentally and everlastingly human.

—**Alain Locke**

The songs of the slaves represent the sorrows of his heart; and he is relieved by them, only as an aching heart is relieved by its tears.

—**Frederick Douglass**

This is one of the glories of man, the inventiveness of the human mind and the human spirit: Whenever life doesn't seem to give us vision, we create one.

—**Lorraine Hansberry**

The function of the music is to raise both performer and audience far above routine emotion; the elderly throw away their sticks and dance.

—**John Lovell Jr.**

Gospel music in those days of the early 1930s was really taking wing. It was the kind of music colored people had left behind them down south and they liked it because it was just like a letter from home.

—Mahalia Jackson

The Cotton Club—smack dab in the middle of Harlem—but Black people couldn't go there. It was for whites only. The club featured Black entertainment and some of the most gorgeous Black women that could be found.

—Joe Louis

The memory of things gone is important to a jazz musician. Things like old folks singing in the moonlight in the backyard on a hot night or something said long ago.

—Louis Armstrong

My mother wanted me to be a star and I worked hard for her goal.

—Lena Horne

I can't express myself in easy conversation—the words just don't come out right. But when I get up on stage—well, that's my whole life. That's my religion.

—Jimi Hendrix

I just came here to entertain you. That was what I thought you wanted. I was born here.

—**Nat "King" Cole, after being beaten on stage
by a group of white supremacists
in Birmingham, Alabama**

I wouldn't sing to segregated audiences, so I sang in Negro schools and white people came.

—**Paul Robeson**

The day I no longer go on stage will be the day I die.

—**Josephine Baker**

Music is your own experience, your thoughts, your wisdom. If you don't live it, it won't come out of your horn. They teach you there's a boundary line to music. But, man, there's no boundary line to art.

—**Charlie Parker**

When I'm on stage, I'm trying to do one thing: bring people joy. Just like church does. People don't go to church to find trouble, they go there to lose it.

—**James Brown**

Got to give us what we want
Gotta give us what we need
Our freedom of speech is freedom or death
We got to fight the powers that be

—**Public Enemy, "Fight the Power"**

Nothing can harm me when I'm on stage—nothing. That's really me. That's what I'm here to do. I'm totally at home on stage. That's where I live. That's where I was born. That's where I'm safe.

—**Michael Jackson**

Black music has always been the prologue to social change.

—**Quincy Jones**

Hip-hop, much as the blues and jazz did in past eras, has compelled young people of all races to search for excitement, artistic fulfillment, and even a sense of identity by exploring the black underclass.

—**Christopher John Farley**

I felt in a lot of instances I was deliberately being put through stress because when you're a guy who generates money, people have a vested interest in controlling you.

—**Dave Chappelle**

I hope I can create art that helps people heal. Art that makes people feel proud of their struggle. Everyone experiences pain, but sometimes you need to be uncomfortable to transform. Pain is not pretty, but I wasn't able to hold my daughter in my arms until I experienced the pain of childbirth!

—**Beyoncé Knowles-Carter**

I think that if we continue to separate ourselves as black or white artists then we separate ourselves from a larger audience. I just happen to be black, which I feel is an attribute, but it shouldn't be an issue. Art has to be more universal.

—**Mildred Howard**

I do know my art's going to be around a long time after I'm gone. That's all you can hope for. That your life made an impact. In a positive way.

—**Spike Lee**

I'm not a Negro tennis player. I'm a tennis player.

—**Althea Gibson**

I've hit 755 home runs, and I did it without putting a needle in my arm or a whiskey bottle in my mouth.

—**Hank Aaron**

After I came home from the 1936 Olympics with my four medals, it became increasingly apparent that everyone was going to slap me on the back, want to shake my hand, or have me up to their suite. But no one was going to offer me a job.

—Jesse Owens

At the beginning of the World Series of 1947, I experienced a completely new emotion when the National Anthem was played. This time, I thought, it is being played for me, as much as for anyone else. This is organized major league baseball, and I am standing here with all the others, and everything that takes place includes me.

—Jackie Robinson

The greatest challenge I faced in becoming a neurosurgeon was believing it was possible.

—Alexa Canady

Curious that we spend more time congratulating people who have succeeded than encouraging people who have not.

—Neil deGrasse Tyson

To build a successful business, you must start small and dream big. In the journey of entrepreneurship, tenacity of purpose is supreme.

—Aliko Dangote

I had to make my own living and my own opportunity. But I made it! Don't sit down and wait for the opportunities to come. Get up and make them.

—Madam C. J. Walker

Always know there is unlimited power in a developed mind and a disciplined spirit. If your mind can conceive it and your heart can believe it, you can achieve it.

—Jesse Jackson

In order to succeed you have to do well and perform well. Don't do less and accept less. Put in the time and complete the task. You want to be a contributing member to every group you are part of.

—Jeanette Epps

We can transcend the script of a pre-defined story, and pave the way for the future that we design. We just need to tap that power, that conviction, that determination within us.

—Robert F. Smith

For every one of us that succeeds, it's because there's somebody there to show you the way out.

—Oprah Winfrey

Success has to do with deliberate practice. Practice must be focused, determined, and in an environment where there's feedback.

—**Malcolm Gladwell**

Growing up I wasn't the richest, but I had a rich family in spirit. Standing here with nineteen championships is something I never thought would happen. I went on a court just with a ball and a racket and with a hope.

—**Serena Williams**

If I can't work with you, I will work around you.

—**Annie Easley**

Dedicate yourself to a core set of values. Without them, you will never be able to find personal fulfillment, and you will never be able to lead effectively.

—**Kenneth Chenault**

The basketball thing: it's fun, I love it. I enjoy it. But to give back, being able to open up a school; that's something that'll last for way beyond my years.

—**LeBron James**

Champions aren't made in gyms. Champions are made from something they have deep inside—a desire, a dream, and a vision. They have to have the skill and the will. But the will must be stronger than the skill.

—**Muhammad Ali**

I am where I am because of the bridges that I crossed. Sojourner Truth was a bridge. Harriet Tubman was a bridge. Ida B. Wells was a bridge. Madam C. J. Walker was a bridge. Fannie Lou Hamer was a bridge.

—**Oprah Winfrey**

Do you see the consequences of the way we have chosen to think about success? Because we so profoundly personalize success, we miss opportunities to lift others onto the top rung . . . We are too much in awe of those who succeed and far too dismissive of those who fail.

—**Malcolm Gladwell**

I don't have big dreams. I just want to be here in five years, breathing and doing what I love to do. I just need to be free to tell my stories from my spirit, my heart . . . unrestricted. Life is fleeting. If we could be here doing what we love to do, that is success.

—**Ava DuVernay**

HARDSHIP, ADVERSITY, AND HOPE

If there is no struggle, there is no progress.

—Frederick Douglass

Why did God make me an outcast and a stranger in mine own house?

—W. E. B. Du Bois

No race or people ever got upon its feet without severe and constant struggle, often in the face of the greatest discouragement.

—Booker T. Washington

The struggle never seems to stop. It gets sharper and sharper.

—Paul Robeson

The challenge for every prisoner, particularly every political prisoner, is how to survive prison intact, how to emerge from prison undiminished.

—Nelson Mandela

There is no better than adversity. Every defeat, every heartbreak, every loss, contains its own seed, its own lesson on how to improve your performance next time.

—**Malcolm X**

I'm sick and tired of being sick and tired.

—**Fannie Lou Hamer**

I had never in my life been abused by whites, but I had already become as conditioned to their existence as though I had been the victim of a thousand lynchings.

—**Richard Wright**

It's not the load that breaks you down. It's the way you carry it.

—**Lena Horne**

My grandmother was a maid and she worked for white folks her whole life. And her idea of having a big dream was to have white folks who at least treated her with some dignity, who showed her a little bit [of] respect. And she used to say, I hope you get some good white folks that are kind to you.

—**Oprah Winfrey**

When suffering knocks at your door and you say there is no seat left for him, he tells you not to worry because he has brought his own stool.

—Chinua Achebe

Many rivers to cross,
But I can't seem to find my way over.

—Jimmy Cliff, "Many Rivers to Cross"

I didn't have anybody, really, no foundation in life, so I had to make my own way. Always, from the start. I had to go out in the world and become strong, to discover my mission in life.

—Tina Turner

I've seen how the broken criminal justice system can really devastate people's lives. I've seen the desperation of people when they want to do the right thing after they come home from prison, like get a job—they're willing to do any type of work. I've had people grab me, pleading with me to help them find employment so they wouldn't have to go back to those nonviolent drug crimes that got them in trouble in the first place.

—Cory Booker

God, make me so uncomfortable that I will do the very thing I fear.

—Ruby Dee

Where I grew up—I grew up on the north side of Akron, lived in the projects. So those scared and lonely nights—that's every night. You hear a lot of police sirens, you hear a lot of gunfire. Things that you don't want your kids to hear growing up.

—LeBron James

You should never view your challenges as a disadvantage. Instead, it's important for you to understand that your experience facing and overcoming adversity is actually one of your biggest advantages.

—Michelle Obama

Overcoming adversity not only makes you stronger, it makes you more hopeful.

—Valerie Jarrett

Success is to be measured not so much by the position that one has reached in life as by the obstacles which he has had to overcome while trying to succeed.

—Booker T. Washington

I never thought of losing, but now that it's happened, the only thing is to do it right. That's my obligation to all the people who believe in me. We all have to take defeats in life.

—Muhammad Ali

I learned that courage was not the absence of fear, but the triumph over it. The brave man is not he who does not feel afraid, but he who conquers that fear.

—**Nelson Mandela**

It's a hurtful place, the world, in and of itself. We don't need to add to it. And we're in a place now where we all need one another, and it's going to get rougher.

—**Prince**

Our ancestors are an ever-widening circle of hope.

—**Toni Morrison**

It is easy to be hopeful in the day when you can see the things you wish on.

—**Zora Neale Hurston**

Hope in the face of difficulty, hope in the face of uncertainty, the audacity of hope: In the end, that is God's greatest gift to us, the bedrock of this nation, a belief in things not seen, a belief that there are better days ahead.

—**Barack Obama**

All human wisdom is summed up in two words—"wait and hope."

—Alexandre Dumas

While there's life, there's hope.

—Terence

Where there is hope there is life, where there is life there is possibility and where there is possibility change can occur.

—Jesse Jackson

WOMEN AND MEN

Next to God we are indebted to women, first for life itself, and then for making it worth living.

—Mary McLeod Bethune

We are free to say that in respect to political rights, we hold women to be justly entitled to all we claim for men.

—Frederick Douglass

That man . . . says that women need to be helped into carriages, and lifted over ditches, and to have the best place everywhere. Nobody ever helps me into carriages, or over mud puddles, or gives me any best place, and ain't I a woman? . . . I have plowed, and planted, and gathered into barns, and no man could head me—and ain't I a woman? I could work as much and eat as much as a man (when I could get it), and bear the lash as well—and ain't I a woman? I have borne thirteen children and seen them most all sold off into slavery, and when I cried out with a mother's grief, none but Jesus heard—and ain't I a woman?

—Sojourner Truth

To be Black and be a woman. To be a double outsider, to be twice oppressed, to be more than invisible.

—Julius Lester

I am glad to see that men are getting their rights, but I want women to get theirs, and while the water is stirring I will step into the pool.

—Sojourner Truth

I am a feminist and what that means to me is much the same as the meaning of the fact that I am Black: it means that I must undertake to love myself and to respect myself as though my very life depends upon self-love and self-respect.

—June Jordan

True chivalry respects all womanhood. . . . Virtue knows no color lines, and the chivalry which depends upon complexion of skin and texture of hair can command no honest respect.

—Ida B. Wells

I'm a woman. I'm a black woman. I'm a poor woman. I'm a fat woman. I'm a middle-aged woman. And I'm on welfare. In this country if you're any one of those things, you count less as a person. If you're all those things, you just don't count, except as a statistic. I am a statistic.

—Johnnie Tillmon

The difference between white and black females seemed to me an eminently satisfactory one. White females were ladies, said the sign maker, worthy of respect. And the quality that made ladyhood worthy? Softness, helplessness, and modesty—which I interpreted as a willingness to let others do their labor and their thinking. Colored females, on the other hand, were women—unworthy of respect, independent, and immodest.

—Toni Morrison

Historically, women have not had ownership of our own bodies. And it is enough. It is enough. You do not get to touch my body or comment on my body as you please. Period.

—Tracee Ellis Ross

Black womanhood is outraged and humiliated. Black womanhood cries for dignity and restitution and salvation. Black womanhood wants and needs protection and keeping and holding. Who will assuage her indignation? Who will keep her precious and pure? Who will glorify and proclaim her beautiful image? To whom will she cry rape?

—Abbey Lincoln

Feminism is just an idea. It's a philosophy. It's about the equality of women in all realms. It's not about man-hating. It's not about being humorless. We have to let go of these misconceptions that have plagued feminism for forty, fifty years.

—Roxane Gay

Defining myself, as opposed to being defined by others, is one of the most difficult challenges I face.

—**Carol Moseley Braun**

I merged those two words black and feminist because I was surrounded by black women who were very tough and who always assumed they had to work and rear children and manage homes.

—**Toni Morrison**

The problem with gender is that it prescribes how we should be rather than recognizing how we are. Imagine how much happier we would be, how much freer to be our true individual selves, if we didn't have the weight of gender expectations.

—**Chimamanda Ngozi Adichie**

I need to see my own beauty and to continue to be reminded that I am enough, that I am worthy of love without effort, that I am beautiful, that the texture of my hair and that the shape of my curves, the size of my lips, the color of my skin, and the feelings that I have are all worthy and okay.

—**Tracee Ellis Ross**

I am not free while any woman is unfree, even when her shackles are very different from my own.

—**Audre Lorde**

Black Girl Magic is a rallying call of recognition. Embedded in the everyday is a magnificence that is so easy to miss because we're so mired in the struggle and what society says we are.

—Ava DuVernay

I think I can inspire a lot of young women to be themselves and that is half the battle. Just be yourself, it's the easiest thing to be. Black girls, we just on another level.

—Rihanna

Every Black woman in America lives her life somewhere along a wide curve of ancient and unexpressed anger.

—Audre Lorde

Being a part of this reemergence of a movement both pro-diversity and pro-woman is the best part of being a Black girl. It's more than "I stand for this because I should." I stand for this because this is part of who I am as a human being.

—Yara Shahidi

When you're a black woman, you seldom get to do what you just want to do; you always do what you have to do.

—Dorothy Height

I was raised to be an independent woman, not the victim of anything.

—**Kamala Harris**

Abandon the cultural myth that all female friendships must be bitchy, toxic, or competitive. This myth is like heels and purses—pretty but designed to slow women down.

—**Roxane Gay**

You've got to learn to leave the table when love's no longer being served.

—**Nina Simone, "You've Got to Learn"**

Guided by my heritage of a love of beauty and a respect for strength—in search of my mother's garden, I found my own.

—**Alice Walker**

I am a strong black woman. I cannot be intimidated, and I'm not going anywhere.

—**Maxine Waters**

I am a feminist. Women are discriminated against in so many ways, and they make up half the population.

—**John Legend**

There's something so special about a woman who dominates in a man's world. It takes a certain grace, strength, intelligence, fearlessness, and the nerve to never take no for an answer.

—**Rihanna**

The success of every woman should be the inspiration to another. We should raise each other up. Make sure you're very courageous: be strong, be extremely kind, and above all be humble.

—**Serena Williams**

You have the power to change perception, to inspire and empower, and to show people how to embrace their complications, and see the flaws, and the true beauty and strength that's inside all of us.

—**Beyoncé Knowles-Carter**

We are the women who marched from cotton fields into fields of medicine, politics, law, education, entertainment. We even found a way to march ourselves into the White House.

—**Jada Pinkett Smith**

I may be a little grayer than I was eight years ago, but this is what a feminist looks like.

—**Barack Obama**

I am an example of what is possible when girls, from the very beginning of their lives, are loved and nurtured by people around them.

—**Michelle Obama**

I believe feminism is grounded in supporting the choices of women even if we wouldn't make certain choices for ourselves.

—**Roxane Gay**

One's sense of manhood must come from within.

—**Martin Luther King Jr.**

Every man is trying to live up to his father's expectations or make up for his mistakes. In my case, both things might be true.

—**Barack Obama**

In those days men left their women for all sorts of reasons . . . and nobody blamed them much, because times were hard.

—**Rita Dove**

There will always be men struggling to change, and there will always be those who are controlled by the past.

—**Ernest J. Gaines**

Being a black man in America is like having another job.

—**Arthur Ashe**

It frightens me that our young black men have a better chance of going to jail than of going to college.

—**Johnnie L. Cochran Jr.**

I am convinced that the black man will only reach his full potential when he learns to draw upon the strengths and insights of the black woman.

—**Manning Marable**

Black men struggle with masculinity so much. The idea that we must always be strong really presses us all down—it keeps us from growing.

—**Donald Glover**

Do you have "the talk" with your kids to warn them within an inch of their lives not to sass the police for fear that they will return home to you in a body bag? I don't mean the usual conversation all parents have with their kids about respecting the cops. Sheer terror and outright fear motivate our discussions.

—**Michael Eric Dyson**

No matter what the professional talkers tell you, I never met a black boy who wanted to fail.

—**Ta-Nehisi Coates**

I'm very proud to be black, but black is not all that I am. That's my cultural historical background, my genetic makeup, but it's not all of who I am nor is it the basis from which I answer every question.

—**Denzel Washington**

Black men who have succeeded have an obligation to serve as role models for young men entrapped by a vicious cycle of poverty, despair, and hopelessness.

—**Benjamin Hooks**

SPIRITUALITY, MORALITY, AND VALUES

'Twasn't me, 'twas the Lord. I always told him, "I trust to you. I don't know where to go or what to do, but I expect You to lead me," and he always did.

—**Harriet Tubman**

I believe in order to understand.

—**St. Augustine**

Any religion that professes to be concerned with the souls of men and is not concerned with the slums that damn them, and the social conditions that cripple them, is a dry-as-dust religion.

—**Martin Luther King Jr.**

I love the pure, peaceable, and impartial Christianity of Christ: I therefore hate the corrupt, slaveholding, women-whipping, cradle-plundering, partial, and hypocritical Christianity of this land.

—**Frederick Douglass**

Religion without humanity is poor human stuff.

—Sojourner Truth

It is this belief in a power larger than myself and other than myself which allows me to venture into the unknown and even the unknowable.

—Maya Angelou

We are close to this earth and to God. Shut up in ghettos, sneered at, beaten, enslaved, we always have answered our oppressors with brave singing, dancing, and laughing. Our greatest eloquence, the pith of the joy and sorrow in our unbreakable hearts, comes when we lift up our faces and talk to God, person to person. Ours is the truest dignity of man, the dignity of the undefeated.

—Ethel Waters

My religion has come to mean more to me than ever before. I have come to believe more and more in a personal God—not a process, but a person, a creative power with infinite love who answers prayers.

—Martin Luther King Jr.

I feel a real kinship with God, and that's what has helped me pull out of the problems I've faced. . . . Through the years, no matter how much success I achieved, I never lost my faith in God.

—Aretha Franklin

My hope for my children must be that they respond to the still, small voice of God in their own hearts.

—**Andrew Young**

My mother gave me something to live on if she weren't around—spirituality and faith. She gave me her base, her spiritual base, her unshakeable base.

—**Gladys Knight**

I remember when I got married, I stopped reading the Bible. When my mother found out that I had stopped, she told me that one should not stop reading the Bible; there was always something new to learn by reading it. On that day, I started back reading the Bible and have not stopped since.

—**Rosa Parks**

Christianity can never be a merely personal matter. It has public consequences and we must make public choices.

—**Desmond Tutu**

To be a Christian is to have a joyful attitude toward the resurrection claim, to stake one's life on it, and to rest one's hope upon its promise—the promise of a new heaven and new earth.

—**Cornel West**

I have read in Plato and Cicero sayings that are wise and very beautiful; but I have never read in either of them: Come unto me all ye that labor and are heavy laden.

—St. Augustine

I am a Muslim and . . . my religion makes me be against all forms of racism. It keeps me from judging any man by the color of his skin. It teaches me to judge him by his deeds and his conscious behavior. And it teaches me to be for the rights of all human beings, but especially the Afro-American human being, because my religion is a natural religion, and the first law of nature is self-preservation.

—Malcolm X

There's no religion in this country that is more misunderstood, miscategorized, and misidentified than Islam.

—W. Kamau Bell

Treating others as you want to be treated. Requiring much from those who have been given so much. Living by the principle that we are our brother's keeper. Caring for the poor and those in need. These values are old. They can be found in many denominations and many faiths, among many believers and among many non-believers. . . . And they're the ones that have defined my own faith journey.

—Barack Obama

Over the years my religion has changed and my spirituality has evolved. Religion and spirituality are very different, but people often confuse the two. Some things cannot be taught, but they can be awakened in the heart. Spirituality is recognizing the divine light that is within us all. It doesn't belong to any particular religion; it belongs to everyone.

—**Muhammad Ali**

I conceive of God, in fact, as a means of liberation and not a means to control others.

—**James Baldwin**

It is my belief that in the Presence of God, there is neither male nor female, white nor black, Gentile nor Jew, Protestant nor Catholic, Hindu, Buddhist, nor Moslem, but a human spirit stripped to the literal substance of itself before God.

—**Howard Thurman**

Not only are we in the universe, the universe is in us. I don't know of any deeper spiritual feeling than what that brings upon me.

—**Neil deGrasse Tyson**

The values of the world we inhabit and the people we surround ourselves with have a profound effect on who we are.

—**Malcolm Gladwell**

Show me your friend and I will show you your character.

—**African proverb**

Character, not circumstances, makes the man.

—**Booker T. Washington**

In fact, because I do not believe that religious people have a monopoly on morality, I would rather have someone who is grounded in morality and ethics, and who is also secular, affirm their morality and ethics and values without pretending that they're something they're not. They don't need to do that. None of us need to do that.

—**Barack Obama**

One of the truest tests of integrity is its blunt refusal to be compromised.

—**Chinua Achebe**

I have learned that as long as I hold fast to my beliefs and values— and follow my own moral compass—then the only expectations I need to live up to are my own.

—**Michelle Obama**

POVERTY AND RICHES

Extreme poverty anywhere is a threat to human security everywhere.

—**Kofi Annan**

Poverty: a hellish state to be in. It is no virtue. It is a crime.

—**Marcus Garvey**

To be a poor man is hard, but to be a poor race in a land of dollars is the very bottom of hardships.

—**W. E. B. Du Bois**

It is easy to romanticize poverty, to see poor people as inherently lacking agency and will. It is easy to strip them of human dignity, to reduce them to objects of pity.

—**Chimamanda Ngozi Adichie**

I never had a chance to play with dolls like other kids. I started working when I was six years old.

—**Billie Holiday**

[W]e were Poor. I'm spelling it with a capital P . . . we were on the bottom of the ladder looking up at everyone else. Nothing below us 'cept the ground.

—Ray Charles

Anyone who has ever struggled with poverty knows how extremely expensive it is to be poor; and if one is a member of a captive population, economically speaking, one's feet have simply been placed on the treadmill forever. One is victimized, economically speaking, in a thousand ways.

—James Baldwin

The burden of poverty isn't just that you don't always have the things you need, it's the feeling of being embarrassed every day of your life, and you'd do anything to lift that burden.

—Jay-Z

The greatest thing I ever was able to do was give a welfare check back.

—Whoopi Goldberg

It's easy to be independent when you've got money. But to be independent when you haven't got a thing—that's the Lord's test.

—Mahalia Jackson

Affluence separates people. Poverty knits 'em together. You got some sugar and I don't; I borrow some of yours. Next month you might not have any flour; well, I'll give you some of mine.

—**Ray Charles**

I've seen a lot of poverty—coming up as a young child, lost hopes and dreams and people that never had a chance to have a decent quality of life. I believe we can do a lot greater than that.

—**Maxine Waters**

I used to think something was wrong with me because I never understood that I was poor. I never understood that I was having to struggle, because the way I thought, I really wasn't. I thought I had it all. I was so much at peace and I was so much into the total surroundings of my family, my grandparents, my mother, and the true love, the true essence of the word "love." I didn't know what all that other stuff was until they passed.

—**Bernie Mac**

When you ain't got no money, you gotta get an attitude.

—**Richard Pryor**

Poverty makes people angry, brings out their worst side.

—**Prince**

As kids we didn't complain about being poor; we talked about how rich we were going to be and made moves to get the lifestyle we aspired to by any means we could. And as soon as we had a little money, we were eager to show it.

—Jay-Z

Everybody in the ghetto aspires to get out. Nobody with sense wants to live there with rats, roaches, crime, and drugs.

—Ice-T

Poverty is not about color.

—Queen Latifah

Do not value money for any more nor any less than its worth; it is a good servant but a bad master.

—Alexandre Dumas

Money is the root of every mess you can think of. There's some folks who would kill you for a nickel. Those are the sorriest folks of all. Anyone who lives for money is surely missing the best things in life. There's satisfaction in doing, in helping. There's an old saying, "Money is useful, but don't let it use you."

—A. Elizabeth Delany

Money, it turned out, was exactly like sex; you thought of nothing else if you didn't have it and thought of other things if you did.

—James Baldwin

If your family doesn't have much money, I want you to remember that in this country, plenty of folks, including me and my husband, we started out with very little. Though with a lot of hard work and a good education, anything is possible, even becoming president. That's what the American dream is all about.

—Michelle Obama

You can only become truly accomplished at something you love. Don't make money your goal. Instead, pursue the things you love doing, and then do them so well that people can't take their eyes off you.

—Maya Angelou

I wanted to become rich and famous simply so no one could evict my family again.

—James Baldwin

The greatness of a man is not in how much wealth he acquires, but in his integrity and his ability to affect those around him positively.

—Bob Marley

Overcoming poverty is not a task of charity, it is an act of justice. Like slavery and apartheid, poverty is not natural. It is man-made and it can be overcome and eradicated by the actions of human beings. Sometimes it falls on a generation to be great. You can be that great generation. Let your greatness blossom.

—Nelson Mandela

I've been rich and I've been poor and I have to admit that rich is better. I'm from the welfare rolls of Chicago, and poverty is always with me. It's what gets me up early in the morning and it is what keeps me up late at night.

—Jack H. Johnson

America doesn't respect anything but money . . . What our people need is a few millionaires.

—Madam C. J. Walker

I am grateful for the blessings of wealth, but it hasn't changed who I am. My feet are still on the ground; I'm just wearing better shoes.

—Oprah Winfrey

I can't help the poor if I'm one of them
So I got rich and gave back, to me that's the win-win.

—Jay-Z, "Moment of Clarity"

I don't like money actually, but it quiets my nerves.

—**Joe Louis**

Only prosperity looks backward. Adversity is afraid to look over its own shoulder.

—**Alain Locke**

WISDOM AND INSPIRATION

Teach your children they are direct descendants of the greatest and proudest race who ever peopled the earth.

—**Marcus Garvey**

We live in a world which respects power above all things. Power, intelligently directed, can lead to more freedom. Unwisely directed, it can be a dreadful, destructive force.

—**Mary McLeod Bethune**

The battles that count aren't the ones for gold medals. The struggles within yourself—the invisible, inevitable battles inside all of us—that's where it's at.

—**Jesse Owens**

To build a better world we need to replace the patchwork of lucky breaks and arbitrary advantages today that determine success—the fortunate birth dates and the happy accidents of history—with a society that provides opportunities for all.

—**Malcolm Gladwell**

Always know that there is unlimited power in a developed mind and a disciplined spirit. If your mind can conceive it and your heart can believe it, you can achieve it. Suffering breeds character; character breeds faith, and in the end, faith will prevail. Armed with this knowledge and a faith in God, you can turn minuses into pluses; you can turn stumbling blocks into stepping-stones.

—Jesse Jackson

I want you to find strength in your diversity. Let the fact that you are black or yellow or white be a source of pride and inspiration to you. Draw strength from it. Let it be someone else's problem, but never yours. Never hide behind it or use it as an excuse for not doing your best.

—Colin Powell

When we drop fear, we can draw nearer to people, we can draw nearer to the earth, we can draw nearer to all the heavenly creatures that surround us.

—bell hooks

The important thing is to realize that no matter what people's opinions may be, they're only just that—people's opinions. You have to believe in your heart what you know to be true about yourself. And let that be that.

—Mary J. Blige

Deal with yourself as an individual worthy of respect, and make everyone else deal with you the same way.

—**Nikki Giovanni**

Do not bring people in your life who weigh you down. And trust your instincts . . . good relationships feel good. They feel right. They don't hurt. They're not painful. That's not just with somebody you want to marry, but it's with the friends that you choose. It's with the people you surround yourselves with.

—**Michelle Obama**

It isn't where you came from; it's where you're going that counts.

—**Ella Fitzgerald**

Nothing the future brings can defeat a people who have come through three hundred years of slavery and humiliation and privation with heads high and eyes clear and straight.

—**Paul Robeson**

The only time we should look back to yesterday is to look at the positive things that were accomplished to encourage us to do better things today and tomorrow.

—**Stevie Wonder**

Trust yourself. Think for yourself. Act for yourself. Speak for yourself. Be yourself. Imitation is suicide.

—**Marva Collins**

There is a way to look at the past. Don't hide from it. It will not catch you if you don't repeat it.

—**Pearl Bailey**

I am especially glad of the divine gift of laughter; it has made the world human and lovable, despite all its pain and wrong.

—**W. E. B. Du Bois**

If I'd known I was going to live this long, I'd have taken better care of myself.

—**Eubie Blake**

Avoid fried meats which angry up the blood. If your stomach disputes you, lie down and pacify it with cool thoughts. Keep the juices flowing by jangling around gently as you move. Go very light on the vices, such as carrying on in society. The social ramble ain't restful. Avoid running at all times. Don't look back. Something might be gaining on you.

—**Satchel Paige**

Take advantage of every opportunity; where there is none, make it for yourself, and let history record that as we toiled laboriously and courageously, we worked to live gloriously.

—**Marcus Garvey**

Fear of something is at the root of hate for others, and hate within will eventually destroy the hater. Keep your thoughts free from hate, and you need have no fear from those who hate you.

—**George Washington Carver**

If you are going to achieve excellence in big things, you develop the habit in little matters. Excellence is not an exception, it is a prevailing attitude.

—**Colin Powell**

Make your success work to help others achieve their measures of success and hope they, in turn, will do likewise. This is the kind of chain reaction that is music to my ears.

—**Berry Gordy**

I thought I could change the world. It took me a hundred years to figure out I can't change the world. I can only change Bessie. And honey, that ain't easy either.

—**A. Elizabeth Delany**

You are where you are today because you stand on somebody's shoulders. And wherever you are heading, you cannot get there by yourself. If you stand on the shoulders of others, you have a reciprocal responsibility to live your life so that others may stand on your shoulders. It's the quid pro quo of life. We exist temporarily through what we take, but we live forever through what we give.

—Vernon Jordan

Once you have experienced a failure or a disappointment, once you've analyzed it and gotten the lessons out of it—dump it.

—Colin Powell

I tell my students, it's not difficult to identify with somebody like yourself, somebody next door who looks like you. What's more difficult is to identify with someone you don't see, who's very far away, who's a different color, who eats a different kind of food. When you begin to do that then literature is really performing its wonders.

—Chinua Achebe

Living in the moment means letting go of the past and not waiting for the future. It means living your life consciously, aware that each moment you breathe is a gift.

—Oprah Winfrey

Seek out people who don't agree with you. That will teach you to compromise. It will also help you, by the way, if you get married.

—**Barack Obama**

Don't let anyone rob you of your imagination, your creativity, or your curiosity.

—**Mae Jemison**

Believe in life! Always human beings will live and progress to greater, broader, and fuller life.

—**W. E. B. Du Bois**

When you are deciding on next steps, next jobs, next careers, further education, you should rather find purpose than a job or a career. Purpose crosses disciplines. Purpose is an essential element of you. It is the reason you are on the planet at this particular time in history. Your very existence is wrapped up in the things you need to fulfill. Whatever you choose for a career path, remember the struggles along the way are only meant to shape you for your purpose.

—**Chadwick Boseman**

We need you to roll up your sleeves. We need to get to work. Because remember this: When they go low, we go high.

—**Michelle Obama**

You really can change the world if you care enough.

—**Marian Wright Edelman**

My humanity is bound up in yours, for we can only be human together.

—**Desmond Tutu**

Now let us begin. Now let us rededicate ourselves to the long and bitter—but beautiful—struggle for a new world.

—**Martin Luther King Jr.**

CONTRIBUTORS

Hank Aaron *(b. 1934)* — American professional baseball player

Kareem Abdul-Jabbar *(b. 1947)*—American professional basketball player, writer, and activist

Chinua Achebe *(1930–2013)*—Nigerian professor, critic, and writer of novels and poetry

Chimamanda Ngozi Adichie *(b. 1977)*—Nigerian activist and writer of novels, short stories, and non-fiction

Alvin Ailey *(1931–1989)*—American choreographer and activist

Muhammad Ali *(1942–2016)*—American professional boxer, humanitarian, activist, and philanthropist

Marian Anderson *(1897–1993)*—American opera singer and activist

Maya Angelou *(1928–2014)*—American poet, writer, singer, and activist

Kofi Annan *(1938–2018)*—Ghanaian diplomat

Louis Armstrong *(1901–1971)*—American trumpeter, composer, singer, and actor

Arthur Ashe *(1943–1993)*—American professional tennis player

St. Augustine *(354–430)*—African-born Bishop and Doctor of the Church

Pearl Bailey *(1918–1990)*—American actress and singer

Ella Baker *(1903–1986)*—American civil rights activist

Josephine Baker *(1906–1975)*—American-born French singer, dancer, activist, and French Resistance agent

James Baldwin *(1924–1987)*—American writer, social critic, and activist

Charles Barkley *(b. 1963)*—American professional basketball player and sports analyst

W. Kamau Bell *(b. 1973)*—American comedian and television host

Halle Berry *(b. 1966)*—American actress

Mary McLeod Bethune *(1875–1955)*—American educator, stateswoman, philanthropist, humanitarian, and activist

Eubie Blake *(1883–1983)*—American pianist, composer, and lyricist

Mary J. Blige *(b. 1971)*—American singer, songwriter, rapper, and actress

Charles M. Blow *(b. 1970)*—American journalist and commentator

Cory Booker *(b. 1969)*—American politician and activist

Chadwick Boseman *(b. 1977)*—American actor

Toni Braxton *(b. 1967)*—American singer, songwriter, and actress

Donna Brazile *(b. 1959)*—American political strategist, analyst, and writer

Claude Brown *(1937–2002)*—American lawyer and writer

James Brown *(1933–2006)*—American singer, songwriter, dancer, and producer

Blanche K. Bruce *(1841–1898)*—American politician

Tarana Burke *(b. 1973)*—American civil rights activist

LeVar Burton *(b. 1957)*—American actor, director, writer, and activist

Octavia E. Butler *(1947–2006)*—American science fiction writer

Alexa Canady *(b. 1950)*—American neurosurgeon

Stokely Carmichael *(1941–1998)*—Trinidadian-born civil rights leader

George Washington Carver *(c. 1864–1943)*—American scientist, botanist, educator, and inventor

Dave Chappelle *(b. 1973)*—American comedian, actor, writer, and producer

Ray Charles *(1930–2004)*—American singer-songwriter, musician, arranger, and bandleader

Kenneth Chenault *(b. 1951)*—American business executive

Charles W. Chesnutt *(1858–1932)*—American writer, educator, lawyer, and political activist

Alice Childress *(1912–1994)*—American playwright and actor

Shirley Chisholm *(1924–2005)*—American educator, politician, and writer

Eldridge Cleaver *(1935–1998)*—American writer and activist

Jimmy Cliff *(b. 1948)*—Jamaican musician, multi-instrumentalist, singer, and actor

Peter Clifton *(unknown)*—Former slave from Winnsboro, South Carolina, whose experiences as a slave were recorded during the 1930s by the Federal Writers' Project of the WPA

Ta-Nehisi Coates *(b. 1975)*—American writer, journalist, and educator

Johnnie L. Cochran Jr. *(1937–2005)*—American lawyer and writer

Nat "King" Cole *(1919–1965)*—American singer, jazz pianist, actor, and activist

Marva Collins *(1936–2015)*—Educator and reformer

James Cone *(b. 1938)*—Scholar, writer, and theologian

Aliko Dangote *(b. 1957)*—Nigerian business magnate

Angela Davis *(b. 1944)*—American activist, professor, and writer

Benjamin Davis Jr. *(1912–2002)*—American military leader

Ossie Davis *(1917–2005)*—American actor, writer, director, activist

Sammy Davis Jr. *(1925–1990)*—American dancer, singer, musician, comedian

Ruby Dee *(1922–2014)*—American actress, poet, playwright, screenwriter, journalist, and activist

A. Elizabeth Delany *(1891–1995)*—American physician and writer

Sarah Louise Delany *(1889–1999)*—American educator and writer

David Dinkins *(b. 1927)*—American lawyer and politician

Frederick Douglass *(1818–1895)*—American orator, writer, editor, and abolitionist leader

Rita Dove *(b. 1952)*—American poet, writer, and professor

W. E. B. Du Bois *(1868–1963)*—American scholar, sociologist, educator, and writer

Alexandre Dumas *(1802–1870)*—French writer

Kevin Durant *(b. 1988)*—American professional basketball player

Ava DuVernay *(b. 1972)*—American film director, producer, screenwriter, marketer, and distributor

Michael Eric Dyson *(b. 1958)*—American scholar, minister, writer, and professor

Annie Easley *(1933–2011)*—American computer scientist, mathematician, and rocket scientist

Marian Wright Edelman *(b. 1939)*—American lawyer, activist, writer, and founder of the Children's Defense Fund

Duke Ellington *(1899–1974)*—American composer, pianist, and bandleader

Ralph Ellison *(1914–1994)*—American writer, literary critic, and scholar

Jeanette Epps *(b. 1970)*—American aerospace engineer and NASA astronaut

Christopher John Farley *(b. 1966)*—Jamaican-born American journalist, writer, and editor

Ella Fitzgerald *(1917–1996)*—American singer and songwriter

Aretha Franklin *(1942–2018)*—American singer, songwriter, and musician

John Hope Franklin *(1915–2009)*—American writer, historian, and scholar

Ernest J. Gaines *(b. 1933)*—American writer and professor

Marcus Garvey *(1887–1940)*—American leader of the Black Nationalism and Pan-Africanism movements

Alicia Garza *(b. 1981)*—American activist and editorial writer

Henry Louis Gates Jr. *(b. 1950)*—American scholar, historian, professor, writer, and filmmaker

Roxane Gay *(b. 1974)*—American writer of fiction and nonfiction, professor, editor, and commentator

Althea Gibson *(1927–2003)*—American professional tennis player

Nikki Giovanni *(b. 1943)*—Writer of poetry and prose, activist, and educator

Malcolm Gladwell *(b. 1963)*—English-born Canadian journalist, writer, and speaker

Donald Glover *(b. 1983)*—American writer, actor, comedian, producer, director, and rapper

Whoopi Goldberg *(b. 1955)*—American actress, comedian, writer, and talk-show host

Berry Gordy *(b. 1929)*—American record executive and music, film, and television producer

Elijah Green *(unknown)*—Former slave from Charleston, South Carolina, whose experiences as a slave were recorded during the 1930s by the Federal Writers' Project of the WPA

Lani Guinier *(b. 1950)*—American civil rights theorist and professor

Bryant Gumbel *(b. 1948)*—American television journalist and sportscaster

Fannie Lou Hamer *(1917–1977)*—American activist, community organizer, and civil rights leader

Lorraine Hansberry *(1930–1965)*—American playwright and activist

Kamala Harris *(b. 1964)*—American lawyer and politician

Dorothy Height *(1912–2010)*—American educator and activist

Jimi Hendrix *(1942–1970)*—American guitarist, singer, and songwriter

Anita Hill *(b. 1956)*—American attorney and professor

Lauryn Hill *(b. 1975)*—American singer, rapper, songwriter, record producer, and actress

Eric Holder *(b. 1951)*—American attorney who served as Attorney General of the United States

Billie Holiday *(1915–1959)*—American jazz singer and songwriter

bell hooks (Gloria Jean Watkins) *(b. 1952)*—American writer and activist

Benjamin Hooks *(1925–2010)*—American minister, attorney, and civil rights leader

Lena Horne *(1917–2010)*—American singer, dancer, actress, and activist

Mildred Howard *(b. 1945)*—American artist

Nathan Huggins *(1927–1989)*—American historian, writer, and professor

Langston Hughes *(1902–1967)*—American poet, novelist, playwright, and activist

Zora Neale Hurston *(1891–1960)*—American writer and anthropologist

Ice-T (Tracy Lauren Marrow) *(b. 1958)*—American musician, rapper, songwriter, actor, and record executive and producer

Jesse Jackson *(b. 1941)*—American civil rights activist, minister, and politician

Mahalia Jackson *(1912–1972)*—American singer and actress

Michael Jackson *(1958–2009)*—American singer, songwriter, dancer, and entertainer

John E. Jacob *(b. 1934)*—Civil rights leader and corporate executive

Harriet Jacobs (Linda Brent) *(1813–1897)*—Escaped slave who wrote *Incidents in the Life of a Slave Girl*

LeBron James *(b. 1984)*—American professional basketball player and philanthropist

Valerie Jarrett *(b. 1956)*—American businesswoman and former government official and presidential advisor

Jay-Z (Shawn Carter) *(b. 1969)*—American rapper, songwriter, record producer, and entrepreneur

Mae Jemison *(b. 1956)*—American engineer, physician, and astronaut

Jack H. Johnson *(1918–2005)*—American businessman and publisher

Jack Johnson *(1878–1946)*—American professional boxer

James Weldon Johnson *(1871–1938)*—American writer, educator, lawyer, diplomat, and activist

James Earl Jones *(b. 1931)*—American actor

Quincy Jones *(b. 1933)*—American musician and record and film producer

Solomon Jones *(b. 1967)*—American writer, journalist, and radio host

Barbara Jordan *(1936–1996)*—American lawyer, educator, politician, and civil rights activist

June Jordan *(1936–2002)*—Caribbean-American writer, educator, and activist

Michael Jordan *(b. 1963)*—American professional basketball player and business mogul

Vernon Jordan *(b. 1935)*—American business executive and civil rights activist

Colin Kaepernick *(b. 1987)*—American professional football player and activist

Alicia Keys *(b. 1981)*—American singer, songwriter, and pianist

John O. Killens *(1916–1987)*—American writer, editor, and professor

Coretta Scott King *(1927–2006)*—American writer, activist, and civil rights leader

Martin Luther King Jr. *(1929–1968)*—American minister and prominent leader of the civil rights movement

Gladys Knight *(b. 1944)*—American singer and songwriter

Beyoncé Knowles-Carter *(b. 1981)*—American singer, songwriter, dancer, actress, and businesswoman

Sara Lawrence-Lightfoot *(b. 1944)*—American sociologist and professor

Spike Lee *(b. 1957)*—American director, producer, writer, actor, and professor

John Legend *(b. 1978)*—American singer, songwriter, and actor

Julius Lester *(1939–2018)*—American writer, folk musician, activist, and educator

John Lewis *(b. 1940)*—American politician and civil rights leader

Abbey Lincoln *(1930–2010)*—American jazz singer, songwriter, and actress

LL Cool J (James Todd Smith) *(b. 1968)*—American rapper, actor, writer, and entrepreneur

Alain Locke *(1885–1954)*—American writer, philosopher, and educator

Audre Lorde *(1934–1992)*—Caribbean-born American writer, poet, and activist

Joe Louis *(1914–1981)*—American heavyweight boxing champion

John Lovell Jr. *(1907–1974)*—American writer

Joseph Lowery *(b. 1921)*—American minister and civil rights leader

Bernie Mac *(1957–2008)*—American actor and comedian

Malcolm X *(1925–1965)*—American religious leader and human rights activist

Nelson Mandela *(1918–2013)*—South African political leader, activist, humanitarian, philanthropist, and lawyer

Manning Marable *(1950–2011)*—American professor

Bob Marley *(1945–1981)*—Jamaican singer-songwriter and activist

Thurgood Marshall *(1908–1993)*—American lawyer and Supreme Court Justice

Claude McKay *(1890–1948)*—Jamaican-born American writer and poet

DeRay Mckesson *(b. 1985)*—American civil rights activist and former school administrator

Kelly Miller *(1863–1939)*—American mathematician, sociologist, writer, and journalist

Toni Morrison *(b. 1931)*—American novelist, essayist, editor, and professor

Carol Moseley Braun *(b. 1947)*—American diplomat, politician, and lawyer

Gloria Naylor *(1950–2016)*—American novelist

Trevor Noah *(b. 1984)*—South African comedian, writer, political commentator, and television host

Barack Obama *(b. 1961)*—American lawyer, writer, politician, activist, and humanitarian who served as the 44th President of the United States

Michelle Obama *(b. 1961)*—American lawyer, writer, activist, and humanitarian who served as the First Lady of the United States

Jesse Owens *(1913–1980)*—American track-and-field Olympic champion

Satchel Paige *(1906–1982)*—American professional baseball player in the Negro Leagues and Major League Baseball

Charlie Parker *(1920–1955)*—American jazz saxophonist and composer

Gordon Parks *(1912–2006)*—American photographer, writer, musician, composer, and director

Rosa Parks *(1913–2005)*—American civil rights activist

Deval Patrick *(b. 1956)*—American politician, lawyer, writer, and businessman

Jordan Peele *(b. 1979)*—American actor, writer, comedian, film director, and producer

Amy (Chavis) Perry *(unknown)*—Former slave from Charleston, South Carolina, whose experiences as a slave were recorded during the 1930s by the Federal Writers' Project of the WPA

William Pickens *(1881–1954)*—American orator, educator, journalist, and editor

Ann Plato *(c. 1820–unknown)*—American writer and educator

Sidney Poitier *(b. 1927)*—Bahamian-American actor, director, writer, activist, and diplomat

Adam Clayton Powell Jr. *(1908–1972)*—American minister, politician, and activist

Colin Powell *(b. 1937)*—American statesman and four-star general in the United States Army

Prince (Prince Rogers Nelson) *(1958–2016)*—American singer, songwriter, musician, record producer, and filmmaker

Richard Pryor *(1940–2005)*—American comedian, actor, and writer

Public Enemy *(1986–present)*—Influential and politically active hip-hop group led by Chuck D and Flavor Flav

Queen Latifah (Dana Owens) *(b. 1970)*—American rapper, songwriter, actress, and producer

A. Philip Randolph *(1889–1979)*—American leader in the civil rights movement, labor movement, and socialist party

Condoleezza Rice *(b. 1954)*—American political scientist, diplomat, and professor

Rihanna (Robin Rihanna Fenty) *(b. 1988)*—Barbadian singer, songwriter, actress, and businesswoman

Paul Robeson *(1898–1976)*—American actor, singer, and activist

Bill "Bojangles" Robinson *(1878–1949)*—American dancer and actor

Jackie Robinson *(1919–1972)*—American professional baseball player who was the first African American to play in Major League Baseball in the modern era

Tracee Ellis Ross *(b. 1972)*—American actress, model, comedian, director, and activist

Wilma Rudolph *(1940–1994)*—American track-and-field Olympic champion

Bill Russell *(b. 1934)*—American professional basketball player

The Scottsboro Boys—Andy and Leroy Wright, Olen Montgomery, Ozie
Powell, Charlie Weems, Clarence Norris, Haywood Patterson, Eugene
Williams, and Willie Roberson; collectively known as "The Scottsboro
Boys." These young African-American men were arrested and charged
with raping two white women in 1931. After cursory trials with no
effective representation, all defendants were found guilty and sentenced
to death. Though the Supreme Court ruled the defendants' due process
had been denied and overturned the death penalties, the cases were
retried in state court and five of the nine defendants were falsely
convicted and served between six and nineteen years in prison.

Yara Shahidi *(b. 2000)*—American actress and model

Al Sharpton *(b. 1954)*—American minister and social justice activist

Nina Simone *(1933–2003)*—American singer, songwriter, pianist, arranger,
and activist

Jada Pinkett Smith *(b. 1971)*—American actress, singer, songwriter, and
businesswoman

Robert F. Smith *(b. 1962)*—American businessman and philanthropist

Will Smith *(b. 1968)*—American actor, film producer, and rapper

Dorothy S. Strickland *(b. 1933)*—American writer and professor

Terence *(195–159 BC)*—Roman playwright

Mary Church Terrell *(1863–1954)*—American activist and educator

Howard Thurman *(1899–1981)*—American scholar, writer, orator, educator,
and theologian

Johnnie Tillmon *(1926–1995)*—American welfare rights activist

Opal Tometi *(b. 1984)*—Nigerian-American writer, activist, and community
organizer

Sojourner Truth *(c. 1797–1883)*—American abolitionist, women's rights
activist, and orator

Harriet Tubman *(c. 1820–1913)*—American abolitionist, suffragist, and
Union scout and spy during the Civil War

Nat Turner *(1800–1831)*—American slave who led a two-day slave revolt in
August of 1831

Tina Turner *(b. 1939)*—American singer-songwriter, actress, and dancer

Desmond Tutu *(b. 1931)*—South African anti-apartheid and human rights activist, theologian, and retired Anglican bishop

Neil deGrasse Tyson *(b. 1958)*—American astrophysicist, writer, and speaker

Alice Walker *(b. 1944)*—American writer of novels, poetry, and short stories; activist

Madam C. J. Walker *(1867–1919)*—American entrepreneur, philanthropist, and activist

Fats Waller *(1904–1943)*—American pianist, singer, composer, and songwriter

Booker T. Washington *(1856–1915)*—American educator, writer, orator, and advisor to U.S. presidents

Denzel Washington *(b. 1954)*—American actor, director, and producer

Kerry Washington *(b. 1977)*—American actress

Ethel Waters *(1896–1977)*—American singer and actress

Maxine Waters *(b. 1938)*—American politician

Faye Wattleton *(b. 1943)*—American educator and activist

Ida B. Wells *(1862–1931)*—American journalist, editor, suffragist, and activist

Cornel West *(b. 1953)*—American minister, professor, writer, and activist

Serena Williams *(b. 1981)*—American professional tennis player

Vanessa Williams *(b. 1963)*—American singer, songwriter, actress, and activist

Walter E. Williams *(b. 1936)*—American economist, commentator, and professor

August Wilson Jr. *(1945–2005)*—American playwright

Oprah Winfrey *(b. 1952)*—American talk show icon, writer, producer, actress, philanthropist, humanitarian, activist, and publisher

Stevie Wonder *(b. 1950)*—American singer, songwriter, instrumentalist, producer, and activist

Carter G. Woodson *(1875–1950)*—American scholar, writer, historian, and founder of the Association for the Study of African American Life and History; known as "the Father of Black History"

Richard Wright *(1908–1960)*—American writer of novels, poetry, essays, and short stories

Andrew Young *(b. 1932)*—American politician, diplomat, and activist